M000279544

BSA

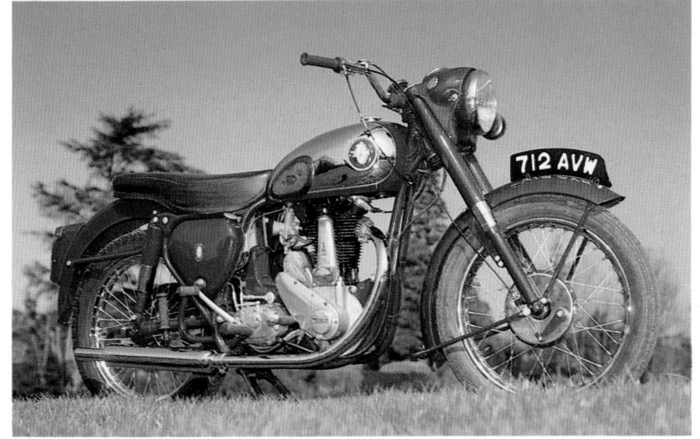
712 AVW

BSA
BANTAM
BSA

CLASSIC MOTORCYCLES

DON MORLEY

My grateful thanks go to the true enthusiasts who so kindly allowed me to photograph their bikes, and also my apologies, since there are too many of them to mention individually.

Thanks also to Alan Williams of the Imperial War Museum for searching through their archives for suitable photographs, and to Rick Howard and Gladys Jones who likewise helped fill some of the more difficult pictorial gaps.

Joy Emerson deserves a particular mention for sorting out my spelling and typing this manuscript, and last although most certainly not least, may I thank both Nicholas Collins and Ian Penberthy of Osprey, without whom this book could not have appeared.

Don Morley
June 1990

First published in Great Britain in 1991 by Osprey, a division of Reed Books, Michelin House, 81 Fulham Road, London SW3 6RB and Auckland, Melbourne

Reprinted Summer 1993, Autumn 1997

Cataloguing in Publication Data for this title is available from the British Library

ISBN 1 85532 118 1

Editor Ian Pemberthy
Page design Paul Kime

Printed in Hong Kong

Front cover
David Roper astride the ex-Dick Mann racing machine

Back cover
The author with a Gold Star from his collection

Page 1
Over engineered? Maybe, but then nothing ever failed, broke, or fell off, which is precisely why the 'B' series springers are in such demand still

Contents

Introduction

My introduction to BSA, and indeed motorcycling, came on a summer's day in 1951 when a friend suggested we pool resources to purchase a 1929 ohv 500 cc Sloper, for which the vendor was asking the princely sum of £2. In those days that was a real fortune to a couple of schoolboys whose combined savings, newspaper round wages and general borrowings still left us four shillings short.

Fortunately, the owner either took pity on us or couldn't find any other mugs, as a cut-price deal was struck. Naturally, there were no other monies left for taking care of the legal niceties, such as driving licences, road tax and insurance, but we reasoned that these were irrelevant since we were under-age anyway. However, we were concerned about how to raise more money for petrol.

Of course, the old bike was long past its best, but in our imaginations it was a Gold Star with which we would surely make our names as famous racers. We did, in fact, become infamous in the eyes of the local law, who only rode BSA pushbikes themselves and who were not overly impressed.

You see, our illegal riding took place around the local cricket pitch where, with the Sloper being decidedly front heavy and the rear tyre being totally bald, we found it child's play (literally) to ride it in speedway fashion with the back end stepping out luridly sideways all around the boundary. This seemed great fun at the time, but our enthusiasm was not shared by the local park keeper.

We should have realized that word of our nocturnal activities was bound to reach the ears of the law eventually, but we didn't, until the night they caught us, that is. They charged us with riding a motor vehicle in a public place without due care and attention, and minus its lights, horn, brakes and silencer, and with not having driving licences or insurance.

Now as if that little lot wasn't bad enough, there was actually much worse to come, for as the police explained, somewhat gleefully, the resulting Court summonses would not go to us, as we were juveniles, but directly to our fathers. Mine happened to be both anti-motorcycling and a rather big fellow. Furthermore, he had not been told about our Beesa's existence!

Recalling the consequences is painful to this very day as, indeed, is remembering our being obliged to dump the Sloper on the nearest refuse tip, never to be seen by us again. However, not even this temporary hiccup changed the fact that we were now motorcyclists for life (as even my father eventually came to realize and respect).

Neither my old mate nor I have even ridden a Sloper since, let alone owned one. However, the M20 and then a pre-war 1000 cc V-twin, plus ten assorted later A7s, Star Twins, Gold Flashes, four B31s, a dozen Gold Stars and three Rocket Gold Stars that have subsequently occupied my garage must say something at least about my long and continuing love affair with Beesas.

There have also been some 18 C15Ts, trials BB34s and B40s, plus several scrambles Victors, all owned and ridden in a 35-year-long competitive riding career, and they are quite apart from the vast number of other people's bikes ridden during my time in professional motorcycling journalism, the tally of which includes even more BSAs.

That latter career involved spells working on the old weekly 'Blue-un' (*The Motor Cycle*) and *Motor Cycle News*, where one was actually paid to travel worldwide whilst covering motorcycling's sports scene, or to road-test most of each era's new products. To me, it all added up to the life of my dreams.

Not all of the many BSAs I rode rated as being perfect for the job or beyond criticism, but there were very few indeed that weren't superbly engineered and better suited than most. May this book be regarded as my small tribute to the men who once made the motorcycles of Small Heath, for as is obvious to this day, they always turned out wonderfully-built and ultra-reliable products.

The early 1950s and the author with his 'raceyfled' A7 rigid of 1947 vintage

BSA: birth and death of a legend

Some 150 years ago, a group of 14 craftsmen gunsmiths in Birmingham found themselves caught up in the Industrial Revolution's technology race. Progress in light engineering suddenly had to be catapulted, rather than inched, forward to meet the sudden and unprecedented demands for new weapons.

Thus far, they had made their guns the laborious way, entirely crafted by hand. However, with the Crimean conflict in the mid 1850s being the first truly mechanized war, their clients in the military demanded mass production and completed guns rolling off assembly lines in their thousands.

The most pressing problem for those particular Birmingham craftsmen was that none had either sufficient workshop space or the capital to invest in the necessary machinery to be able to switch to mass production. So in June 1861, they formed a co-operative.

By pooling their resources, they were able to purchase a 25-acre site, on which to erect a purpose-built factory, in what was then rural Small Heath. They christened the previously narrow, unmade approach lane 'Armoury Road' and were soon in production, the new consortium being known as The Birmingham Small Arms Trade.

The original equal-vote partnership proved rather unwieldy, so in 1863 they elected a chairman and reformed as a limited company, primarily to be able to settle impasses through the chairman's casting vote. This new grouping became The Birmingham Small Arms Co. Ltd — BSA.

The company's next great problem, however, was a relatively long period of peace. Such times were not exactly good for gunsmiths, as their main clients, the government, could meet their own needs through making armaments in the Royal Ordnance factories.

Wealthy buyers of sporting guns, meanwhile, tended to shun mass-produced weapons for, ironically, they still favoured the sort of hand craftsmanship for which BSA's founders were previously famous. However, it was too late to turn back the clock, and BSA could not afford to let either its machinery or workers stand idle.

Fortunately, in the late 1870s, a saviour appeared in the form of a well-known eccentric, a Mr. E. Otto, who had invented not a bicycle, but the dicycle. This was rather like the front half of a penny-farthing, but instead of having one large wheel, it had a pair, which were set side by side and belt driven. The rider sat between the wheels whilst steering via a pair of vertical stirrup-type handles, and although this rear-wheel-less ensemble actually looked rather unstable, it worked surprisingly well. This was demonstrated ably by Mr. Otto, to BSA's directors' amazement, when he rode it over the top of their boardroom table, off down the head office stairs and into the distance along Armoury Road.

BSA bought his invention and kept its machinery busy in making over 1000 before going on to lead the field in mass-produced bicycle design. The company's famous 'piled rifles' trademark became accepted throughout the world as a symbol of what was considered to be the very best in British workmanship.

Various rival French and American bicycle manufacturers, meanwhile, had been experimenting with steam instead of pedals for power. However, these new-fangled devices were proving too heavy, and they suffered from a limited range whilst also taking a long time to get up steam, so BSA was not overly impressed.

Not until Gottlieb Daimler and Wilhelm Mayback invented the first benzine-powered internal-combustion engine did Small Heath begin to really take note, although even then, and unlike so many other bicycle makers of the era, BSA did not rush into production. Instead, the company limited its interest to merely testing the profusion of engines available from others.

The announcement of BSA's first true motorcycle came in a rather modest four-line 'Novel and New Models' paragraph which appeared in *Motor Cycling* magazine, dated October 1910. In its entirety, it read, 'The BSA Co. Ltd. are producing a single cylinder motor bicycle on standard lines, a fully illustrated description of which will appear in an early issue'.

Hardly mind blowing, even in those days, but none the less heralding the beginnings of an entirely new era, for from the introduction of that humble 3½ hp belt-driven, single-speed motorcycle followed 60 quite fantastic years. During that time, scarcely a week would pass without one of Small Heath's two-wheelers making history in some part of the world.

Armaments and pedal bikes still accounted for the greater part of the company's business, however, so 1911's motorcycles were produced at a satellite factory in Redditch. Here, a further development soon brought the bike a rear hub clutch which, although adding another £6.10s to the basic £50 price, put it right to the forefront.

A year later came a dual-control two-speed gear hub, and 1913 brought an almost modern countershaft gearbox, along with totally enclosed front and rear drive chains. These features, together with the multi-plate clutch and efficient engine drive shaft shock absorber, meant that this 3½ hp machine was well ahead of its time.

World War I again made enormous demands on BSA's resources, the company supplying literally millions of rifles and machine guns to the combined Allied forces. It also led to previously undreamt profits, so there was no shortage of money to fund the ensuing peacetime motorcycle developments.

The old 3½ hp (499 cc) model continued into 1919 and was joined that year by a larger-engined (557 cc) 4½ hp version. Surprisingly, since BSA was one of

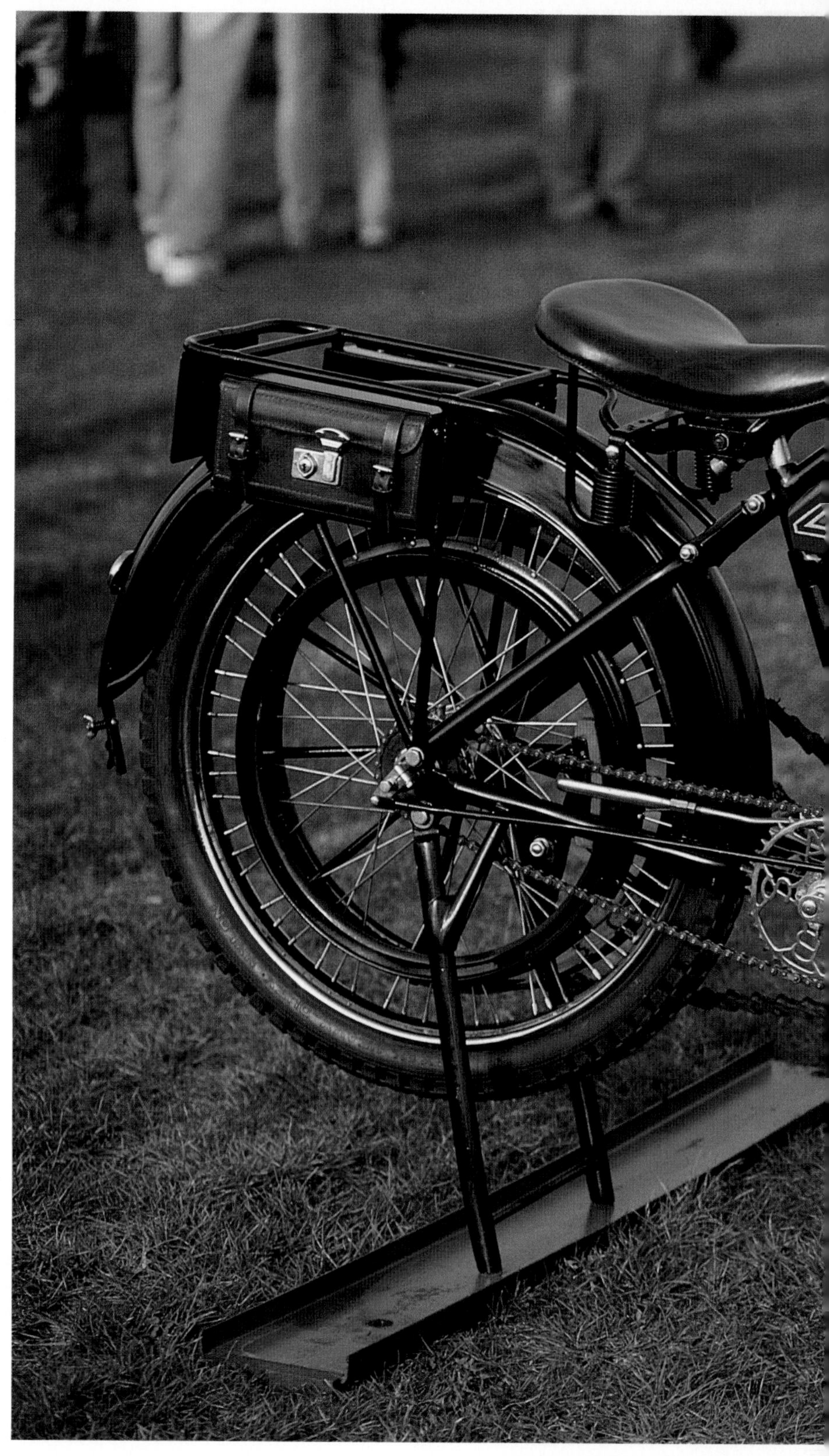

David Gardner's beautifully restored
$3\frac{1}{2}$ hp 1913 model

B.S.A.
CE 1920

26

Above

The year 1914 saw the larger 4 hp job and a countershaft gearbox, so there was no more pedalling

Left

Another $3\frac{1}{2}$ hp of 1913, but this is the 'stripped-for-action' TT version, which is about to be raced at Brooklands

the leading exponents of all-chain drive, it came fitted with old-fashioned belt drives, although for an extra £4 chains could be specified.

For the 1920 season, BSA added a third model which was powered by a new 6-7 hp (770 cc) V-twin engine. The 'stump-pulling', wide-spread of power of this bike was best suited to hauling sidecars, so the company decided to build those as well.

Hence, through the 1920s and beyond, side-valve V-twin BSA sidecar outfits carried entire families and became real workhorses. Many were even used as taxis to haul anything from businessmen or goods to the era's flappers and their escorts on their evenings out on the town. Our local window cleaner was still using his to transport himself, his buckets and ladders in the late 1950s.

There was a new single-speed version of the old 3½ hp machine for 1920 which was rather grandly christened the 'TT' model. However, this title and the bike's low £77 price owed more to the fact that it had merely been stripped down to the basics rather than designed for competition. It should not be confused with 1921's genuine factory racers. Those were duplex framed and even had four-valve cylinder heads, which were especially cast in alloy. Unfortunately, someone at the works hadn't quite done their homework, for although six started in the 1921 TT, none finished. Even when running, none proved particularly fast.

Pausing for a moment from cataloguing BSA's more general history, it is worth pointing out that neither these works racers nor the later, and immortal, post-war Gold Stars were ever shorn of surplus weight. They weren't as delicate as the highly successful, genuine, racers from the likes of Norton, Velocette, AJS, Rudge and Sunbeam.

Instead, BSA built a proud reputation for making long-lasting products, albeit through their engineering being more reminiscent of the Forth Bridge, so by not holding together or staying the distance, those 1921 bikes reaped much scorn. The resulting bad publicity was something that the BSA board decided could not be risked again.

All future racing aspirations were immediately terminated, yet just as the proverbial phoenix rose from the fire some good also came out of this débâcle. In attempting to restore the company's good name—in which they succeeded—BSA turned instead to contesting all other forms of motorcycle sport.

Their number one works trials rider, Harry Perry, also rode a standard 350 cc, round-tank, 1924 two-speeder from the Birmingham factory to Wales. Then, by riding it over the wooden sleepers between the mountain railway lines, he carried on to the top of Mount Snowdon amidst a blaze of publicity.

The actual climb took just 24 minutes from top to bottom, and it was the first time that Snowdon had been conquered by vehicle. On another publicity jaunt, a team of riders carried out a 45,000-mile, multi-terrain trek through 24 countries to prove the machines' reliability. It took them 18 months to complete.

Stunt followed stunt, each carefully aimed at illustrating the product's reliability and strength. although outright speed was quite deliberately rarely

BSA's early 1920s V-twin-engined taxi, in which the passengers sat side by side

B.S.A.

Same model, but with civilian sidecar, photographed in 1982 on Westminster Bridge during the VMCC annual London run

mentioned, not least due to the never-forgotten TT débâcle. BSA had chosen the role of being a high-volume producer of mechanized cart-horses, leaving its rivals to play with the fillies.

BSA's real success during the 1920s and early 1930s came through supplying large numbers of 'bread-and-butter machines to motor agencies, such as the AA and RAC, and other organizations that ordered in relatively high volumes. Surprisingly, this rather impressed Joe Public who, likewise, bought these dependable products to go off and watch the antics of other marques' racers.

Milestone bikes of the era must include 1924's two-speed 250 cc model—as opposed to the large-capacity (350 cc) round-tanker—which became THE commuter bike of its era, and their first two-stroke design which arrived in 1926. This bike featured a 174 cc engine that was very advanced for the period and that actually ran backwards, although this was merely due to it employing a two-pinion geared primary drive. Sadly, despite its modernity earning it a place in history, this model was not overly successful, unlike 1929's four-stroke Sloper.

The Sloper with its inclined engine was a tuned version of the earlier tourer, and to distinguish it from that more mundane model there was a large red star on the fuel tank. Thus began what proved to be an extensive galaxy of ever higher-tuned and image-boosting Blue Stars, Empire Stars, Silver Stars and, finally, Gold Stars, as BSA increasingly moved into the speed market.

If there was anything new to be tried during the 1930s, then BSA tried it, including fluid flywheels and a semi-automatic (pre-selector) transmission. However, come 1939 and the Hitler war, it was back to grass roots, turning out over 16,000 rifles a week, together with machine guns and heavier armaments. BSA also manufactured a grand total of 126,334 military M20 motorcycles which were shipped to virtually every area of conflict.

During the war, the company bought up many lesser factories to be able to expand production, and with a ready eye towards the end of hostilities they also acquired Sunbeam, New Hudson and, finally, Ariel. BSA had become one of British industry's all-time most powerful and profitable conglomerates by the end of the war.

With the end of hostilities, whilst being financially healthier than ever, the company found that, like most others in the industry, it was unable to switch back to motorcycle production in volume due to the acute shortage of raw materials. This led to the industry postponing the resumption of its annual Motorcycle Show because there was nothing to put in this shop window.

This situation continued for three further years, although BSA was better off than most when the materials did start trickling through, as they already had some fairly radical projects which should have been introduced in 1940 had war not intervened. Consequently, they merely needed to blow the dust off these and various other prototypes when that day arrived.

One of these new machines was the 500 cc Herbert Perkins-designed, semi-unit-construction A7 parallel twin, which was unveiled without the aid of a show in 1946. However, this model was intended initially for export only, due to those continuing material shortages. Meanwhile, what should have been the really hot Gold Star version of Wal Handley's pre-war Brooklands racer was not only further delayed, but in the interim it became well watered down.

None the less, BSA's 1947 range did include the cast-iron-engined competition B32 and B34 with, no doubt, the first peacetime Scottish Six Days Trial in mind. Both, together with the 250 cc model C11, 350 cc B31 and the new A7 twin, featured new telescopic front forks instead of the previously traditional girders. The side-valvers of the range, however, hung on to the pre-war type for at least a little while longer.

There was some unofficial activity heralding the arrival of the ZB32 Gold Star racer through a small number of works-prepared prototypes being rather illegally loaned out for use in 1947's Junior Clubmans TT. Entry to this event was supposed to be strictly limited to production machines that already existed, so BSA was bending the rules.

In 1948 six more prototype ZB32s were entered in the Island, that being ridden by A. D. Bassett at one time running third fastest in practice, although in the race itself, all but the last placed, ridden by A. King, went out early on. Given BSA's previous TT racing débâcle, this was precisely why the company

Above
Not sure how BSA's top brass viewed this 1930 Champion advert featuring one of their redoubtable Slopers in trouble, or how many of that period's motorcyclists really rode around in white Oxford bags!

Right
Britain's National Motorcycle Museum now owns the only known A7 Star Twin survivor from 1952's International Six Days Trial trio

BSA
MOL 303
NATIONAL
MOTORCYCLE
MUSEUM
1952 B.S.A. STAR TWIN 500cc.
MAUDES TROPHY MACHINE

was not yet prepared to admit any official involvement.

November 1948 saw BSA unveil what was by far the most comprehensive model range the motorcycling world had ever seen, including the eventual production version of those Gold Star racers and the first of the two-stroke Bantams. On the twin front, there was also a tuned A7 version, called the Star Twin which, as most other models, could be supplied with BSA's new, optional, plunger-type rear suspension.

Hardly a bike had escaped major modification. The single-cylinder B-range machines were all fitted with the M-types' stronger gearboxes, and the M-range, intended for hauling sidecars, were equally brought up to date the addition of telescopic front forks. With the exception of the flywheel-magnetoed Bantam, each model also received an uprated dynamo which allowed the use of a brighter (24 as opposed to 18 watt) bulb in their headlights.

Incidentally, BSA's traditional model letter prefixing might seem rather confusing, especially as some overhead-valve 500s were apparently linked by the 'M' letter to the side-valvers, yet visually appeared to be indistinguishable from the supposedly sportier B-range. The simple explanation for this is that the frames of the ohv-engined M-bikes were fitted with sidecar lugs, whereas the otherwise identical B-types were not.

The era's sporting riders loved the new Star Twin and Gold Star, but it was left to the humble little Bantam to really hit world marketing headlines, for a whole new generation raced, trialed, scrambled and went to work on the bike. It also had many female buyers and, despite the vast numbers produced, those early Bantams achieved almost cult status.

Joe Public didn't go to work on an egg but a Bantam, the post and telegrams were delivered by it, teenagers lusted for it (and the nubile young ladies who had already bought them). Of course, BSA happily obliged by producing tens of thousands, if not actually millions. This couldn't have been bad business for what was really a German (DKW) design which had been liberated by BSA as their spoils of the war.

1949 brought Bert Hopwood's superbly-designed and long-lived 646 cc Golden Flash vertical twin, so loved by soloists and sidecarists alike. Despite its name, which continues to confuse, it came painted black UNLESS the buyer ordered the metallic beige finish (not really gold) and paid an extra £10!

On the amateur sports front, Harold Clark won the 1949 Junior Clubmans TT with a standard production 350 cc Gold Star, the first of BSA's many ensuing victories. In the professional ranks, the company's works-entered trials, enduro and scrambles team, brilliantly led by Bill Nicholson, helped the marque become almost totally dominant through two-and-a-half more decades.

The 500 cc Gold Star entered production late in 1949 for 1950, and at the same time the trials B32s and B34s received much the same alloy cylinders and cylinder heads. Meanwhile, in what was a particularly inspired publicity

The year 1954, and BSA were arguably best, and certainly biggest, in the world, with machines ranging from the little 125 cc commuter Bantam to their mighty 650 cc Gold Flash. The latter was also available with swinging-arm rear suspension by that time, although only for export

quest, BSA invited John McNulty, who represented Britain's Auto Cycle Union, to choose at random three perfectly standard machines from the assembly line in readiness for what would be a rather special test, even by BSA's standards.

McNulty picked the three ohv Star Twins from a batch of 35 built on 30 August 1952. He marked each with seals before locking them away until the test began on 7 September. On that date they were handed to Fred Rist, Brian Martin and Norman Vanhouse who were to ride them under constant supervision, and without any extra preparation, for thousands of really arduous miles.

The route ran from London to Harwich, where they all boarded a ferry bound for Holland, on through that country into Belgium, France, Switzerland, Austria, Germany, Denmark and, finally, Sweden. Here the 'Olympics' of motorcycle off-road sport, the International Six Days Trial, was just about to commence and the three BSAs were entered. Although they were roadsters and far from suited to off-road enduros, each machine and rider proceeded to put in faultless (zero penalty) Gold Medal performances.

Despite the pounding they received on the 4958-mile trip, not one of the machines suffered much more than a blemish. For this incredible feat of skill and reliability, BSA was awarded Britain's prestigious Maude's Trophy.

These bikes were loaned next to *Motor Cycle* magazine, again proving faultless on test, even when compared to identical, but brand-new, machines. Following this, each had its engine stripped under ACU supervision so that every individual component could be inspected and carefully measured. All were found to be within their original manufacturing tolerances and, therefore, virtually perfect.

In their ensuing adverts, BSA claimed: 'It proves once again, as so often demonstrated in the past, the unfailing reliability and high standards of performance for which BSA motor cycles are justly famous all over the world—the sort of reliability and performance which YOU require and can confidently expect when you choose a BSA'.

These adverts also stated: 'It proves beyond all shadow of doubt the superb quality of design, craftsmanship and materials inherent in every BSA model'. What they might also have said, but didn't, was that it had been an incredibly brave, but potentially risky, effort, for by taking along numerous press men as witnesses, the factory also chanced any negative publicity had anything gone wrong!

November 1952's Motor Cycle Show saw this still mud-stained trio of Star Twins in pride of place on BSA's stand, although by this time they were being overshadowed by the near totally revamped Gold Stars. Among many other improvements, these had gained cast-alloy primary chaincases, single-bolt-fitting fuel tanks, new frames with far superior swinging-arm suspension, and the much sweeter gearbox adopted from the A-type twins.

The remaining models in the range received the beautifully-styled one-piece headlamp nacelle which visually neatened the bikes no end, not least as this cowling also contained the speedometer, ammeter, and headlamp switch and all but hid their necessary, but previously conspicuous, multitude of cables and wires. With these models looking so good, my generation literally queued up to buy.

Only the Gold Star and the export version of the Gold Flash were fitted with the new all-welded, swinging-arm frame. This was because BSA had difficulty in adapting its volume manufacturing process from the old lug-and-braze method to lugless-and-welded. Consequently, with the exception of that headlight cowling and a new faired-in rear number plate, all the other models remained much as before.

This home-market situation was partially remedied during 1954 with the release of a mere handful, by BSA's standards, of swinging-arm, as opposed to plunger, Flashes. Then in 1955, when BSA had at last sorted out its frame production problems, the company introduced the new 500 cc swinging-forked Shooting Star model, which replaced the plunger-suspended Star Twin. Similarly, each of the B-group's big solos eventually got a Goldie-type frame.

My own view has always been that those very few 1954 heavyweight swinging-arm jobs, and not so many more surviving 1955 models were, and are, both visually and functionally, quite the best bikes BSA ever made, and that the company commenced its downhill slide with the 1956-on modifications. I have held that opinion, incidentally, despite admitting some exceptions and having ridden so many thousands of working miles on the products that ensued.

For me, BSA spoiled what were the best bikes with their October 1955 (for 1956 production) styling exercise. No doubt, conscious of the era's newly affluent teenagers who, unlike we old stagers, by then bought 44 per cent of ALL mid 1950s products, the company, in what was a flaccid and miserable attempt to 'jazz up' an image, risked the wrath of all experienced bikers.

Lost, for instance, was the much respected (Gold Star-type) single-sided 8 in. front brake, to be replaced by Ariel's puny, though possibly more fashionable, full-width component, which never worked well.

The new matching rear brake, which was operated by a cross-over cable instead of a rod, was spongy and worse, for the cable always tended to stretch which, at least in my hard riding experience, just wasn't progress.

From then onwards, ever more dubious styling exercises regularly came and went, including numerous garish changes to the previously understated, but much loved, fuel tank badges. Furthermore, what had been quite the prettiest headlamp nacelle was replaced by the ugliest. That said, however, there were still some good bikes to come including, had it not been for those same awful new brakes, the pre-unit-construction 650 cc Road Rocket.

What was really happening in this period of changing markets during the mid to late 1950s was a management crisis of confidence. Sadly, this tended to filter down to the workforce who, incidentally, were not over enamoured with either the situation or the extravagant lifestyle of their company's millionaire chairman, Sir Bernard Docker, or even more especially that of his extrovert wife.

My own view and recollection, for what it's worth, is that the Dockers cleverly brought the products of the entire company—which by that time also owned the Triumph motorcycle and Daimler car groups—in front of a far greater audience. Being such glorious publicists, they were rarely, if ever, off international TV screens or newspaper front pages and, in the process, plugged BSA amply, even if it was through something like a gold-plated Daimler.

Beyond question, Sir Bernard and Lady Norah's reign coincided with what was the company's most successful post-war period, in which it produced its best products. Of course, it should also be said that this is equally attributable to the efforts of the company's managing director, James Leek. While shunning much personal publicity, he brilliantly got on with running the 'nuts-and-bolts' end of the business.

Docker was finally kicked out by his fellow directors during 1956, and I, for one still think they were both jealous and wrong, especially as they must have been aware of James Leek's continued ill-health which forced his retirement within weeks of the Dockers' demise. This suddenly left the company without its two top men, drifting like a ship minus its rudder.

June 1956 saw Gold Star-mounted Bernard Codd win the Junior and Senior Clubmans TTs, the first and last time in the event's history that ANY rider scored a double. It wouldn't be repeated because BSA's near total domination of this series post 1947 had become too much of an embarrassment to the various other manufacturers who, being unable to win, had simply withdrawn from competing, leaving a single-marque race.

The 1957 TT organizers' face-saving excuse for calling a halt to the Clubmans races was that they wished to extend the international race distances to eight laps for what was the event's golden jubilee, to which end they needed the amateurs' track time. For 1958, they promised, the series could return and the races revert to their original format.

Not that it happened that way, for once gone, it was quietly forgotten, although the Clubmans events were reconstituted briefly at Silverstone. That exercise, however, was but a continuation of the carve-up, for there was also a rule change to open the doors to the entry of pukka Grand Prix race bikes. Thus, production racing came to an end in the UK and with it the reign of the Gold Star.

Immortal it might have been, but with nowhere to compete, the Goldie was demoted instantly to being a mere café racer, for despite its fantastic Clubmans TT record, it was actually far too heavy and slow to be matched on level terms against the overhead-cam pukka Grand Prix bikes. Ironically, Britain's greatest loss was not so much the Goldie, but its form of racing, which was the breeding ground that helped produce many great international riders, such as Bob McIntyre, Phil Read, Alan Shepherd and John Cooper, to name but a few.

BSA's traditional engineering-trained directors, meanwhile, were also beginning to lose out in the post-James Leek era, as the money men and accountants took over in the company's continuing internal power struggle. This increasingly caused an unhealthy imbalance between those who appreciated, understood and, if only occasionally, rode the products, and those others who only saw beauty in balance sheets rather than in products crafted for the transport and enjoyment of man.

Middle management, even in this dark period, however, remained surprisingly good, but became caught up in the crossfire between their superiors and the highly skilled blue-collar workforce. The latter, in turn, found themselves increasingly obliged to correct a whole series of component design faults, often while suffering from a nonsensical deluge of edicts from above.

To say that labour relations at BSA, by the very late 1950s, were already in tatters would be a considerable understatement, not least illustrated by what happened on one of my own visits to photograph the new C15 model's purpose-built assembly line. My quite inadvertent actions caused the entire workforce to suddenly down tools and walk out on strike.

On arrival, I had been given a long list of do's and don'ts aimed at preventing me from upsetting the workforce which, by then, was easily done. Then I had been left to get on with the job of setting up my lights, camera, tripod, etc, whilst my BSA middle-management escort hospitably nipped off to fetch us some much needed sustenance from their excellent canteen. That was when it all happened.

All had gone well until I switched on the photo floodlights, which coincided with the return of my tea-bearing, but suddenly ashen-faced, friend. On realizing that the workforce had stopped and were muttering he dropped our teas and went down on bended knee to them with the plea that as I wasn't a BSA worker but *Motor Cycle* magazine's staff man, obviously I couldn't have known better, and please would they go back to work.

My heinous crime had been to flick on my own light switch, something that one did dozens of times elsewhere in each working day, but this was not elsewhere stated BSA's shop stewards and the mass walk-out proceeded. Their 'iron-fisted' union's rules demanded that a company electrician should switch on any such lights, making it a very sorry moment for me.

Come the company's centenary in 1961, however, and at least outwardly all seemed reasonably well. A new unit-construction 350, called the B40, had been introduced to replace the old B31 heavyweight, and by giving what was virtually the 650 cc Road Rocket single-sided Goldie-type brakes and rechristening the result the Rocket Gold Star, even that bike at last became what it should always have been.

We motorcyclists of the period still looked upon BSA as being an

712 AVW

My own 100,000+ mile B31 of 1954 vintage. It had the same chassis as the racing Gold Stars, except for the front brake

impregnable pillar of motorcycling society, and were mostly taken in by the claim that of all motorcycles being used anywhere in the world, one in four had been made at Small Heath. Despite BSA's many wrong turns, we overlooked the fact that this 'one in four' business made no mention of how many bikes were being sold annually.

By this time, sales figures for motorcycles were falling off, not least due to Sir Alex Issigonis'cheap and cheerful Mini, which was wooing many youngsters away from two wheels and on to four. BSA's answer was to set up the now infamous Umberslade Hall 'Think Tank'. There, a succession of 'with it' whizz kids, straight from college, were intended to design a new range of products that, hopefully, would tip the scales back in the company's favour.

One suspects that had Umberslade's staff recruitment been limited to those who actually rode motorcycles, it might have worked. Sadly, someone at BSA had obviously overlooked this particular criterion, for there flowed a whole series of designs which, though supposed to appeal to the young because they were by the young, instead often proved utterly impractical, as any experienced rider could have told them.

Umberslade's new frames for 1971, for instance, featured a seat height that was almost too great to climb upon. Other machines might have looked fine when standing upright, but couldn't be safely ridden or cranked over into a corner due to ancillaries such as the exhaust pipes and side or main stands being set so low that they dragged on the ground once the machine was a few degrees off vertical, with the attendant risk of their causing an accident.

Such continuing problems were numerous and varied, often resulting in production delays which, in turn, caused the company to miss critical shipping dates to their main foreign markets. This culminated in the American West and East Coast distributors eventually refusing any further late deliveries, despite the fact that the bikes were on the high seas—most of their customers had long since gone off and bought Japanese machines instead.

Faced with this sudden loss of expected funds, together with the extra cost of shipping the machines back and stockpiling such large numbers of what would soon become dated, surplus American-spec. bikes—or alternatively converting them to meet European tastes in an already lacklustre, overstocked market—BSA was obliged to go cap in hand to the City in search of more finance.

The almost immediate effect of this fight for survival being made public was a sudden drop in the company's share values. At the time, no one thought it a great problem, for this sort of thing happens regularly when any large

NAJ 325

group takes a temporary downturn. However, in the wings was a particularly dangerous predator who saw a chance to make some extra money quickly.

His course of action was to take a chance by purchasing a very large block of marked-down BSA shares, over the telephone, with money he didn't really have. With the company's recovery generally predicted, his plan was to sell again almost immediately in the hope of making a huge profit. All of this was to be achieved before he was obliged actually to pay for their purchase.

For him, I offer no sympathy, as for BSA and the ordinary, unknowing shareholders it all went horribly wrong. Instead of rising, the company's stock values continued to fall, leaving our villain unable to either sell and recoup or pay the original purchase price. This immediately resulted in the stock market suspending any further BSA share dealings pending their official enquiry.

This infamous day was 14 March 1971, and although the fraudster had no official connection with BSA, it caused a large number of suppliers and frightened bankers to decide that perhaps there was 'no smoke without fire'. As a result, they cancelled BSA's normal working credit or demanded their monies in advance of orders, and in the process finally brought down what was otherwise a reasonably healthy empire.

As the shock waves of the demise of this almost Ford-like group literally reverberated around the world, we motorcyclists told ourselves that surely it could only be a temporary hiccup, especially as BSA's products had seemed to be improving and back in demand. However, despite hopes of a long-term rescue, as opposed to asset stripping by Dennis Poore's Norton Villiers empire, this really was the end.

Former TT race star Robin Sherry and Gold Star DB 350 lapping the magic Island – evocative indeed

BSA
BSA

Where did it all go wrong? This early 1970s high-seated Thunderbolt sums up all that was worst of BSA's final years

V-twins

Above
Beautifully engineered and lovely to behold, although rather heavy and lacking in performance, for this is a late 1930s half-litre version

Right
'Used daily all the year round', according to the owner of this 1000 cc job, spotted during 1990 at a Classic Bike Show. Neither he, nor we, should mind the oil leaks, for it has been earning its keep since 1939

FHW
678
1939 B.S.A. 1,000cc
USED DAILY, ALL YEAR ROUND.
JOIN CAM.R.B.! (CAMPAIGN FOR REAL BIKES)
OWNER:-

OHV Slopers

BSA's 493 cc Sloper was the company's first post-1921 bike to break their previous deliberately staid and stolid image, most especially if it was ordered with the £6 optional race kit. This included a higher-compression-ratio piston, inlet and exhaust valves and springs made of better materials, and a small selection of sprockets for increasing the overall gear ratios so as to make the most of the extra brake horsepower.

My own first bike happened to be an S29, the 'S' being for Sloper and '29' indicating its year of manufacture, hence an engine or frame stamped S30 would have been built in 1930, etc, until the model's demise in the mid-1930s. During the same period there were also side-valve and larger-capacity ohv versions.

The tuned ohv 500 had a maximum on tap of about 80 mph, which was quite low when compared to the era's more sporting Sunbeams, Rudges and Nortons, but the inclined engine configuration certainly created a fashion, for this idea was rapidly copied (and often improved) by virtually every other manufacturer.

BSA eventually fitted the tuning kit as standard on one of the 500 cc ohv models, which could be identified externally by a large red star transfer on the fuel tank that formed the backdrop for the marque's more normal three-letter badge. The machines featured here in colour, however, are 'cooking' type Tourers.

When I bought mine, 38 years ago, it was already over 20 years old, but even then it was still greatly revered by one's elders and betters who, unlike me, had been around when these bikes were in current production. Most such men must have passed on now to even greater motorcycling glories, whereas my generation heaped its praise instead on the much later Gold Stars. It is a sobering thought, however, that it's almost 30 years since even that bike's demise.

Quite a late one this, a 1933 600

B.S.A.

Above

The 1930s half-litre benefited from having more chrome on its fuel tank

Right

Not posed, but a 'snatched' picture of an unknown Sloper rider pobbling past, using his bike on a glorious day for exactly the purpose it was made for

B.S.A.

Speedway

BSA got involved with speedway once or twice, but most notably during 1928 when Jack Parker and Cyril Lord helped design, develop, and successfully race what became the company's only officially listed speedway model. This was based around the company's 493 cc Sports Roadster's ohv engine.

Featured here is the reputed development machine actually used by Lord during 1928, from which came the 1929 production dirt tracker priced then at just £65. However, as they were not top sellers, they quietly slipped from BSA's range from 1930.

Incidentally, BSA's final competitive fling was also to have been in speedway with a much modified B50 Victor, developed on that occasion by Arthur Browning and Ray Wilson who used a special Rob North frame. Sadly, Small Heath folded before their highly successful prototypes made it into production.

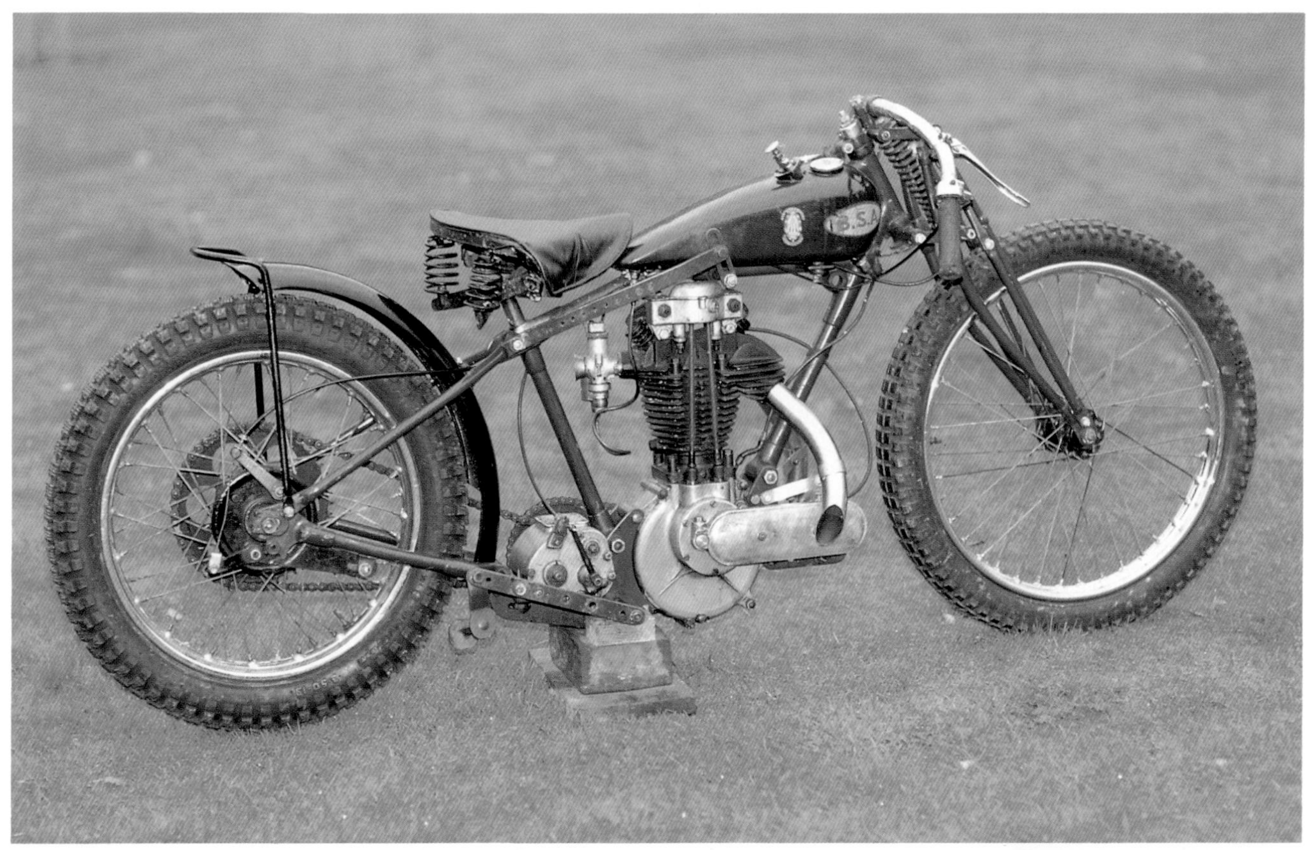

B.S.A.

1930s singles

Val Page, who is better known nowadays for his Ariel designs, moved to BSA during the 1930s, and in a very short space of time gave them the new 'B' and 'M' type engines. These shared many common components regardless of final cylinder capacity, or whether the poppet valves were fitted at the side of the cylinder or above it.

Gone also was BSA's previous practice of casting the oil tank within the forward portion of the engine which, despite their still being dry-sump designs, caused the earlier engines and their chassis to be unnecessarily long. Page's shorter bikes gave better handling.

The new designs first hit the market at the 1936 Motorcycle Show for 1937 production and included a totally revised 250/350/500 cc range of Empire Star sportsters. Other than their name, these machines owed virtually nothing to their predecessors. All enjoyed totally enclosed valve gear, as opposed to only an enclosed inlet as before, and there was a polished cast-alloy tunnel to replace the previous pushrod tubes.

These new Empire Stars featured tuned engines with air-hardened cast-iron cylinder barrels and four-speed gearboxes, which enjoyed enclosed positive-stop foot-change. The entire clutch assembly and pressed tin oil-bath chain case were of new designs that BSA would continue to use on all their other heavyweight models right up until the mid 1950s.

BSA's pre-war model prefixing, however, was no less confusing than its post-war system. The original ohv 'C' range were all 250s, the 'B's were 350s, and the 'M' types all 500s, which might seem logical enough, except that those same three capacity-denoting letters eventually also included the 600 cc side-valvers, and there was also a 350 cc Trials 'C' type!

The prototype M20 500 cc side-valver first saw light as a works-entered trials bike, with which A. E. (Bert) Perrigo won more National Trial Premier Awards during 1937 than any other rider. however, Wal Handley's brilliant Brooklands racing effort that year, on what was another semi-prototype, was surely BSA's greatest pre-war competition highlight. He took a highly-tuned, but still cast-iron-engined, 500 cc Empire Star to the famous banked track and promptly won a three-lap handicap event at a phenomenal, in those days, 102.27 mph average, easily gaining one of Brooklands' coveted Gold Star awards following an incredible best lap of 107.57 mph.

Those Brooklands Gold Stars were only ever given to the few riders and car drivers who lapped the track at speeds of over 100 mph, which even in the late 1930s was still a far from common achievement. Handley's performance was all the more impressive because he was mounted on what was really a 500 cc roadster. Much to the delight of staid old Small Heath, it brought them considerable good publicity.

A beautifully restored light 19 of 493 cc and 1930 vintage

RU
654
B.S.A.
BSA

BSA

Above
BSA's Val Page designed a trials bike for 1939, the B25 Silver Star. It was of 350 cc not 250 cc capacity, as its model number might seem to suggest

Left
Similar to the previous picture, but the opposite side of a machine spotted parked by the roadside during 1990

Right
Officers tended to be more equal than most in Britain's wartime Army. Hence Captain J. H. 'Jimmy' Simpson acquired a 1939 Gold Star rather than the more humble standard-issue M20 for his 1941 despatch rider training duties, but then he was also a former TT winner

37
18

Could almost be period, but this shot was actually taken during 1990 at the Talmag Trial. It features a military model M20 which actually saw World War 2 service in North Africa

The company's resultant trumpet-blowing advert ran: 'BSA eclipses BSA, the brightest chapter in the brilliant history of BSA'. More importantly, to cash in further, they set about building not a replica as it turned out, but a brand-new production version. Albeit based on Handley's machine, it was technically far more advanced.

Handley's bike had actually been a fairly standard Empire Star that had been fitted with a very high-compression-ratio piston to run on alcohol instead of petrol, whereas the supposed replica's engine was given an all-new alloy top end as opposed to the previous bike's cast-iron version. The new model's heritage demanded that it be christened 'Gold Star'.

In fact, there were two 500 cc Gold Star M24 models introduced at the end of 1937. As might be expected, one was for out-and-out speed work, while the other version, which came fitted with an upswept instead of downswept exhaust system, extra clearance mudguards and competition tyres, became BSA's latest trials bike or scrambler.

The production side-valve M20s (500 cc) and M21s (600 cc) similarly made their first public appearance at that same 1937 London show, whereas the older Empire Stars were gradually phased out during 1938, or rather retitled for 1939 as Silver Stars. This merely implied that they were now one step down on the tuning ladder from the later Goldie.

Those final Silver Stars virtually became the post-war B31s and B33s, with the exception of their girder forks, but all such civilian models were lost, however, when in October 1939 BSA switched entirely to painting bikes in khaki.

Some 126,000 military side-valve-engined M20s rather than Gold Stars left Small Heath's production line over the next few years, yet even their Val Page-designed engine bottom halves were nigh on identical to those of Handley's bike, though without quite the same performance!

B31 and B33

If there was one machine that typified all that was so right and good about the heavyweight products of the once British motorcycle industry, then surely BSA's over-engineered, 350 cc, single-cylinder B31 would have to be it. I haven't forgotten its larger-bore, 500 cc brother in making that claim, either.

Both bikes were more or less identical, except for the size of piston, rear chain and tyre, but it was the long-running 350 that was so loved by the motorcycling public and helped make BSA a fortune. It outsold the larger-capacity bike by probably as many as 15 to one.

The reasons for this were the favourable road tax and insurance rate in most countries for 350s, and the fact that they were quite a lot cheaper to buy (which always seemed rather ridiculous bearing in mind these models' extreme similarities and the minimal differences in their performance).

Elders of my generation bought the bulletproof B31s, for each and all of those reasons, and perhaps even more so because the 350, if ridden very carefully, could better 75 mpg. In petrol-rationed early post-war Britain, of course, this was very important.

The B31 introduced in 1945 was also BSA's first ever tele-forked machine, but it was otherwise most closely related to the ill-fated and ultra rare B29, which would have been the company's 1940 mainstay had war not intervened. The very few B29s that were made were promptly requisitioned for use by the military. Their combined fate was to be left behind in Dunkirk when France fell to the Germans. Their eventual B31 replacements also suffered from the ravages of war, although indirectly via the ensuing low-octane (pool) petrol, which demanded it be much less of a sporting bike than its predecessor. BSA had been obliged to fit a lower-compression-ratio piston, softer cam timing and smaller carburettor to suit the era's poor quality fuel.

When petrol did finally improve to a point where, had they so wished, BSA could have made some amendments to the tourers, they didn't bother because they had already brought in the 350 cc Gold Star for the speed men, and added the larger 500 cc B33 at the end of 1947 for 1948 onwards.

Engine prefixes on both models ran through XB (1945–7) to YB (1948 only), then the ZBs took over between 1949 and 1952 (and numerically are most common), followed finally by the BB series. The last encompassed the swinging-arm-framed era up to 1959 and these models' eventual demise.

Plunger rear suspension also became an optional extra from the end of 1949, although few machines with this actually reached the home market, as most of the early versions were destined for export. Surprisingly, this type of suspension never was a standard fitment in the UK on either the B31 or B33 until AFTER the swinging-arm frame's arrival.

Above right
A fairly early post-war period rigid-rear-ended B33, although not so early, for the speedometer is situated on the fork top yolk rather than in the fuel tank

Below right
The 'B' series engines grew deeper cylinder finning by 1953, while the machines had larger fuel tanks and acquired a headlamp nacelle. The 7 in. front brake signifies that this is a B31 rather than a B34

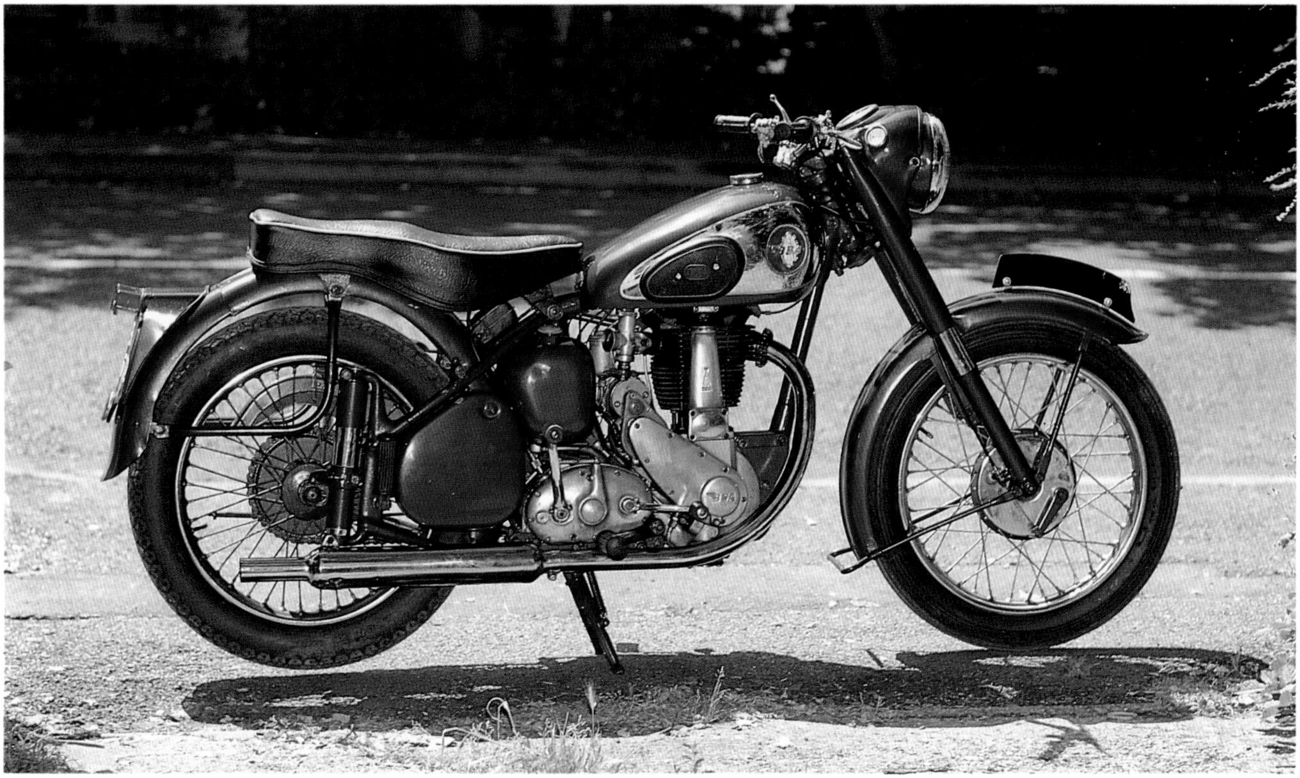

Perhaps BSA were merely trying to use up old, surplus forgings in 1954 when they listed the home-market touring 'B' range with plunger suspension, leaving the foreigners to receive the proper springers, albeit with a very few exceptions, which is why those early swinging-arm jobs were, and are, so rare in the UK.

Fortunately, some 1954–5 swinging-arm 'B' types did escape homewards, and as these virtually shared the racing Gold Star's chassis, they must surely rate as being best of all. The numerically more common 1955-onwards machines were all lumbered first with Ariel's, and later Triumph's, horrible (full-width) brakes.

The B33s of the same period even had the Gold Star or Flash's far superior single-sided, 8 in. front brake/hub, yet both bikes were equally heavy, so the 350 took just as much stopping from similar speeds. It really should have been fitted to both machines, if only on the latter to reduce the many moments of near abject terror!

Performance-wise,there was little difference between the 350 and 500, with about 73 mph on tap for the former and around 80 mph for the latter. However, these bikes weren't about all-out speed, rather they were ultra-reliable, comfortable, cheap-to-run plodders that could be wound up to just a little below their absolute maximum, and then happily left to hold this cruising rate uphill and down. Some 100,000 low-maintenance miles were not at all uncommon for either a B31 or B33 without the big-end ever seeing daylight.

They still retain a considerable charm even in use today, being quite willing to cover high daily mileages with but the occasional drink. Open the throttle hard, mind you, and other than a change in the exhaust note, not a lot happens.

The engine's low state of tune remained pretty nigh identical throughout these models' lifespan, but in becoming ever more comfortable, their chassis suffered increasingly from middle-age spread. Hence there was some loss of performance, for their weights went steadily up from 340 lb (350) and 351 lb (500) to a whopping 410/421 lb at their demise.

We 1950s youngsters used to paint our 'cooking' 'B' type petrol tank, cast-iron barrel and cylinder head silver, kidding ourselves we were really riding Gold Stars. As most of us also fitted the latter bike's sportier touring cams—part nos. 65-2448 (in) and 65-2450 (ex)—along with their stronger matching valve springs, our bikes could become almost as fast.

Why BSA never offered this option from new, as opposed to supplying the parts for later owner fitment remains one of life's little mysteries. Undoubtedly, they transformed the undertuned iron engines with no apparent trade off, turning even the late and heavier type B31s into near enough 90 mph sportsters.

I never did work out how BSA expected this tiny 7 in. front brake to stop over 400 lb of speeding motorcycle

Right
Earliest and best of the B31 swinging-arm jobs, 1954's model, as featured here, came with a shallower front mudguard than the otherwise identical-looking 500. However, both used the deeply valanced version a year later

712 AVW

Bantam: transport for all

BSA's, indeed the entire British industry's, all-time best-selling motorcycle was not a sports model (although there were some mildly sporting derivatives), but rather the humble, ride-it-to-and-from-work, but otherwise forget it, little Bantam. Built down to a price as a three-speed, 123 cc two-stroke for 1949 onwards production, BSA's Bantam instantly caught the public's attention, for at the time petrol was still rationed and these early bikes could easily top 50 mph yet return up to 120 miles for every gallon.

Thus, Bantams were desired equally by cost-cutting big businesses and the man in the street. Consequently, several new generations of motorcyclists cut their teeth on those little D1s, and in the early days, at least, BSA could not keep pace with demand.

The enlarged capacity D3 Bantam Major arrived at the end of 1950 with plunger rear suspension as standard, and 1958 brought the even larger 175 cc engined models with swinging-arm frames. In this ever continuing development process, however, they lost much of their original spartan appeal.

Bantam production continued in volume, none the less, right through until 1971, when the top of the range model was the four-speed D175 with far better front forks, totally redesigned main engine castings, higher cylinder compression ratio, central spark plug and improved clutch. This certainly rated as the best Bantam ever, but by then it was all too late when faced with the superior Japanese products.

Never was an advert more truthful than BSA's for their 1960 Bantam

THE MOTOR CYCLE, 13 APRIL 1950
A charming Australian on her B.S.A. Bantam. This model is becoming increasingly popular in Australia and indeed all over the world.
The BSA
BANTAM
everybody's motor cycle all over the world
VIC 47·785
The District Nurse chooses Bantam because it's dependable
The B.S.A. Bantam 125 c.c. is rapidly becoming known everywhere as "The small machine with the BIG performance". And it is proved performance too.
Recently two standard B.S.A. Bantams, selected from Distributor's stock, underwent an A.C.U.-Observed Test in Australia to prove economy and performance figures. One model averaged 213.3 miles to the gallon over a distance of 200 miles. The other covered 510 miles in 12 hours—averaging 42½ m.p.h. with a fastest lap of 48½ m.p.h.
For lightweight economy and "big-bike" performance the B.S.A. Bantam has no equal.
6-footers can be at their ease astride the Bantam.
Youth gets away to a wonderful start with a Bantam.

A genuine 1949–50 works-specification 123 cc trials Bantam, as developed for the factory by the legendary rider/engineer Bill Nicholson

Countless learners acquired their first riding skills on a Bantam, and in the RAC/ACU's Learner Training Scheme, as being demonstrated during the 1960s by this fellow

Above

The 1966–7 full swinging-arm framed and larger 175 cc engined version – almost the last of its line

Right

A D7 of 1954 complete with plunger rear suspension and optional dualseat

BSA
BANTAM
BSA

Gold Star ZB

Sombre utility was very much the name of the game in November 1948 when Britain's motorcycle industry, devoid of raw materials, was struggling to build even enough bikes to mount their first post-war show, let alone have any left for sale. Many would be exhibiting what really were their mildly updated pre-war models, albeit with additions such as telescopic front forks, and most had to detune their pre-war engine designs because they needed to run on the prevailing low-octane (72°) and very poor quality pool petrol.

No one could even begin to predict the six-day show's likely attendance, for what little there was of that petrol remained strictly rationed, and in war-torn Britain, public transport was very limited. Incredibly, 176, 207 visitors did make it to pack London's Earls Court almost to the rafters which, against the backdrop of travel difficulties was truly incredible. This very grand total almost doubled any similar show's previous pre-war record attendance.

It didn't seem to matter that no one could actually buy anything, or even that there were no startlingly new products expected. What really did count in those heady days of continuing patriotism was that this was peacetime, and the show proof both of Britain's own products and the return of civilian motorcycling.

Everyone seemed caught up in a new atmosphere of optimism, which was further fuelled on the very eve of the show when first BSA, and then Triumph, surprised everyone by unveiling a few new, quite radical and less austere models that not even the press had expected.

Triumph's dual offerings were the fabulous 498 cc Trophy and Grand Prix, while BSA replied with their Bantam, a tuned version of the existing A7 and the Gold Star. The last could be ordered with racing gear ratios, pistons and/or carburettors.

As standard (if you could get one), the Gold Star came with BSA's new plunger rear suspension, employed an ordinary non-racing type Amal carburettor, and was fitted with full lighting and magdynamo, whereas the engine's outer timing cover as yet had no provision for a rev-counter drive.

Certainly, the new bike looked a beauty, especially in those austere days., Among its attractive features were almost flat-section, chrome-plated mudguards and red-lined silver panels on a chromed fuel tank.

One very inadequate feature, which also appeared on all other such big BSAs, was the exceedingly meagre 7 in. front brake. This had already long struggled to slow even the touring machines, yet now it was being asked to stop the faster and, incidentally, appreciably heavier Gold Star.

BSA's new and ultra-heavy rear plungers lay at the root of the bike's considerable weight gain, for they alone more than cancelled out any savings made by the engine's all alloy top-end castings. Unlike the B31 rear suspension, the plungers were standard as opposed to being optional extras.

Below
A ZB Clubmans racer engine restored to its original glory

Above

A rare Gold Star survivor from 1937's 'M' series batch. Note this engine's pushrod tunnel shape compared to that of the revamped post-war 'B' type

Right

The year 1949, and Ray Hallett preparing for that year's Clubmans TT. Note the 7 in. front brake still in use (although fitted with a home-crafted air scoop), the straight-through exhaust pipe, touring handlebars and all-painted fuel tank. The last, no doubt, was fitted to save the precious plated version from accidental damage. Creditably, he finished in fourth place

The actual alcohol-fuelled 1949 ZB 31 campaigned by myself until the mid 1950s, and seen at Alton Towers prior to throwing off the clutch whilst lying in sixth place

The irony of this undamped suspension was that it gave a choppy ride, which often resulted in unpredictable handling. Consequently, many Clubmans TT riders chose to cure those occasionally frightening problems by locking BSA's suspension solid, which rather defeated the object!

BSA announced the arrival of the larger-capacity 500 cc Gold Star in 1949 when, together with the 350, it at last received the new Gold Flash's 8 in. front brake. However, in the UK, the bigger bike went almost ignored, not least in those days because only a 350 could be entered in both race classes. For the less well-heeled, two chances of earning race prize money with only one bike wasn't to be missed.

As an aside, my own racing and scrambling career commenced with a 350 ZB Gold Star, which although a bit long in the tooth when I got it was the machine ridden by Brian Purslow when he actually won the Junior Clubmans TT. Quite apart from running on dope for racing and scrambling, it also had to take me to and from work.

Common practice used to involve us having a spare set of wheels already fitted with scrambling 'knobblies', while the ordinary tyres and wheels were used for both commuting and road racing. The roadster handlebars would be turned up or down, and the footrests and gear lever reversed, as often as necessary. Beyond this, we would do little race preparation, other than occasionally swopping a sprocket.

Cheap, cheerful and usually very happy sporting days they were, too, although my memories of racing early Gold Stars include the fact that they were really built for big men, not ten-stone weaklings like me with size seven feet. Even so, they could be made to fly, especially when running on dope (alcohol) rather than petrol.

My main recollections are of a heavy clutch that over a long race took someone stronger than I to keep pulling in, and of an equally enormously stiff gearbox with an agricultural-feeling foot-change lever, the end of which was always just too far away from my particular toes. All caused regular muscle aches and blisters. One couldn't shorten the gear lever without losing leverage, and slackening the clutch springs only caused it to slip.

I will never forget a 'flat out in third' moment on Alton Towers' long defunct short straight when my bike's clutch decided it was time to self destruct permanently. We were all racing elbow to elbow at the time and bearing down on a 90-degree bend, which also happened to run slightly downhill, when this fully assembled clutch suddenly whizzed past in mid-air

BSA
OCT 90

ahead of me before hitting and then bouncing back off the track, threatening to decapitate more than a few. Several riders went down in the resulting mêlée, and you can probably guess who was the least popular among them. Funny in retrospect is the fact that the errant clutch was not seen again, for by the time we had sorted ourselves out, it had disappeared into the trackside jungle of rhododendrons, and for all I know it's probably still there.

Above
Still titled a ZB for 1952's Clubmans TT races, but already fitted with what would soon become the 1953-onwards BB series upper engine castings

Left
The other side of the same 1952 TT racer, showing this period's rather leaky pressed tin primary chain cases

Competition B32 and B34

Legendary is the only word to adequately describe BSA's 1940s and 1950s works trials team, not least because they literally dominated the sport with bikes that even in those days could hardly be described as 'state of the art'. Yet so great were the talents of Small Heath's riders that they were only very rarely defeated.

The winning machines all stemmed from BSA's production Competition B32, which was introduced in 1946 as a derivative of the rigid-rear-ended B31 roadster. This had been further graced with slightly more ground clearance, wider-ratio gears and a high-level exhaust system. It weighed in at 364 lb dry, which was staggeringly heavy for any trials bike.

In 1949 the larger-capacity B34 (500 cc) version appeared, and both versions received the Gold Star's cast-aluminium cylinder and cylinder-head. However, they did not inherit the latter bike's swinging-arm frame until 1955's model year. Even then the final alloy-engined versions still weighed in too heavily at 336 lb, had an overlong (55¾ in.) wheelbase and suffered from 6¾ in. of inadequate ground clearance (unladen!).

What the B32/34s did have going for them was quite the best trials-suited powerplant in the business, coupled to a sufficiently low centre of gravity to ensure very superior handling, and, of course, those works riders who were capable of winning no matter what they rode.

Hence, on a rough count, works BSA's entered and won 138 National Championship Trials between 1946 and 1958, including the Scottish Six Days (twice), and achieved a quite staggering total of 15 British Experts solo and/or sidecar trial wins. Works riders Bill Nicholson, Jeff (J.V.) Smith, Harold Tozer and Frank Darrieulat between them won the overall British Championships a record nine times for any manufacturer.

Most of the victories were gained on 500s, although Brian Martin preferred, and quite often beat all comers, riding his 350. The Beesa boys more usually than not came away with the equally prestigious Manufacturers' Team Prize, but despite their phenomenal success rate, few privately-mounted B32/B34 runners managed a major win.

BSA

COMPETITION

350 cc. Model B32

500 cc. Model B34

With a most impressive list of premier awards to their credit, gained in Trials and Scrambles in all parts of the world, these two B.S.A. models have proved the most successful post-war competition machines. Lucas magdyno lighting is standard; alternative lighting equipment is available. Spring frame extra (with downswept exhaust pipe only).

With magneto and bulb horn

Model	Price	Tax	Total
B32	£120. 10s.	Tax £32. 10. 10.	Total £153. 0. 10.
B34	£130. 10s.	Tax £35. 4. 8.	Total £165. 14. 8.

With magdyno

Model	Price	Tax	Total
B32	£128.	Tax £34. 11. 3.	Total £162. 11. 3.
B34	£138.	Tax £37. 5. 3.	Total £175. 5. 3.

Prices include Speedometer.

Above

Built like a battleship and almost as heavy, that just about sums up the 1946 iron-engined competition B32/34s. I rode one just once in a trial and decided never again!

Below right

Perhaps this bike's owner felt the same way, for his 1948 B32 was forlornly standing with a 'For sale' notice at 1990's Classic Talmag Trial

4

Above left

Despite being catalogued, very few of 1954's superb duplex-framed, alloy BB-engined comp' jobs actually reached the public, although BSA's works riders won almost everything going on them

Below left

Too long, heavy and low really, yet BSA's short-lived, and nowadays ultra-rare, swinging-arm competition B32/34s of the 1955–7 era were virtually unbeatable in the right hands

Above right

Former BSA works rider and multi Scottish Six Days winner Arthur Lampkin gave his old B34 an airing by riding it again in 1984's Classic One Day Scottish, although after 20 odd years he found it a bit of a struggle!

Below right

Steve Stevens piloting his mid 1950s 350 through Kent mud in a late 1980s trial. Later, a bad leg break sadly ended his competition career

Above

The 500 cc B34 once had few peers as a sidecar trials bike, for such was the available power output that they could be almost guaranteed to bulldoze up, over, or indeed even through, literally anything

Right

A trials sidecar championship-winning B34 from 1957's final production batch, owned and regularly used now by Dave Betteridge. He recently even rode it to and from the Balearic Isles

TERRITORIAL ARMY
M.C.C.
30-4-90

Pre-unit twins

BSA's first parallel twin to enter production was the 500 cc A7 model, which was based on a 1930s Val Page design that had been adjusted and shuffled around by Edward Turner, then honed to near perfection during the war years by Herbert Perkins and David Munro, under the guidance of the equally famous designer Bert Hopwood. Therefore, it is doubtful that any other motorcycle ever had quite such a talented development team, or enjoyed nearly so lengthy a gestation period.

Perhaps the most interesting aspect of the A7 was its semi-unit-construction powerplant, where the separate gearbox was bolted solidly to the engine's crankcases without engine plates, resulting in a particularly rigid assembly that also featured a fixed centre and duplex primary drive chain assembly, which was virtually unique in those days.

The engine's concept really was quite brilliant, and very much in advance of any rival, or even BSA's own later twins, other than the virtually identical early 650 cc A10s. As these powerplants were physically small, it also meant that the bikes could be shorter in wheelbase.

One interesting departure from more normal parallel twin design was BSA's use of a single camshaft, when every other engine of the period used two. Naturally, this reduced the numbers of drive pinions and so almost halved any mechanical backlash or noise. That near uncanny quietness was further ensured by the dynamo being chain driven via a drive shaft which featured an outrigger bearing.

These original twins were, in short, beautifully balanced and virtually vibration free due, not least, to their low state of tune. Mechanically, they were very much quieter than Triumph's twins, whose buffs couldn't hope to emulate the A7 owners' party trick of standing a coin upright on the bike's saddle where it would balance happily all day while the BSA's running engine just tick-tocked away.

In 1949 the mildly-tuned, twin-carburettor, 500 cc A7 Star Twin appeared, and brought with it some loss of smoothness as the price paid for 92 mph as opposed to the 'cooking' version's 88 mph maximum. However, this loss was more than offset by the new bike gaining rear suspension as standard and the Gold Flash's superior 8 in. front brake.

As speeds rose, however, there was increasing doubt over these rear plungers' handling at speed, for there was no damping mechanism whatsoever at the rear end, and BSA's by then fairly archaic front forks had no damping on recoil either. As a result, each end tended to be out of step and clashing with the other.

Roland Pike, meanwhile, débuted a swinging-arm-framed Gold Star in 1952's Senior TT, and although this machine wasn't an official company

Above right
BSA's prototype A7 twin with the silver-painted fuel tank originally intended for production. What's more, its speedometer was fork-top rather than tank-top mounted

Below right
The first plunger-suspension 650 cc A10, as unveiled during 1949 for 1950 production. Note the single casting rocker box, 8 in. front brake and deeply valanced front mudguard

Below
1947's production A7 engine featured a bolt-on gearbox, single forward camshaft, two separate rocker boxes and a slipper-type primary chain tensioner

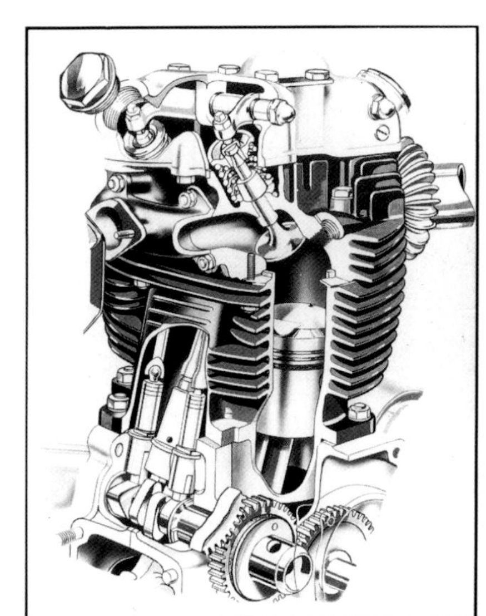

Above

1954's plunger Flash could be considered an interim, or Mk 2, version. It featured a dualseat, faired-in rear number plate and the same headlight nacelle as that year's overlapping swinging-arm job

Left

The A7 tourer for 1952–3 came with the larger-capacity 1950-type Flash fuel tank and was painted maroon

effort, it did have fully-damped rear suspension. He worked in BSA's development department alongside the legendary works rider/engineer Bill Nicholson, whose duties officially included improving the racing bike's handling.

Nicholson built the prototype Gold Star springers that were used so successfully by the British Army in the same year's International Six Days Trial, where BSA's own official team also won three gold medals and the prestigious Maude's Trophy, riding a trio of old plunger-style Star Twins. The Army Gold Stars used engines, gearboxes, etc of pre-unit construction.

BSA might have considered updating the 'B' range's virtually 1920s arrangement of numerous separate engine plates and gearbox-to-primary chain adjustment draw bolts when they finally introduced their new swinging-arm frame. Sadly, however, they took a considerable step backwards by separating the twins' engines from their gearboxes and opting to adapt the single's truly old-fashioned, and inferior, primary transmission.

The excuse for returning to the dark ages of design was that the company would save most money by standardizing transmissions and frames across their entire heavyweight range. However, as the respective engines' shapes proved ultimately incompatible, it didn't work out that way, for BSA were still obliged to make two versions of frame.

(Not until the mid 1960s was this matter really put right, and then only by Small Heath designing an all-new range of fully unit-construction twin-cylinder engines, but they tended to vibrate rather badly and one wonders what might have happened had they only come up with the post-1964 short-wheelbase frames for use with the superior semi-unit type powerplants.)

One of 1952's tuned A7 Star Twins, and rare indeed now

All that really counted, however, was how the package worked, and those resulting 1954–5 twins should go down on that count as being quite the best 'all-rounder' bikes that Britain ever made. Not only were their engines superb, despite the previous criticisms, but now they also handled.

BSA progressively spoiled their post-1955 bikes through the addition of full-width hubs whose brakes never worked as well, and then a wholly needless succession of styling changes of usually inferior taste. The one brilliant exception to this rule was the 650 cc Rocket Gold Star.

Nowadays, it is no coincidence whatsoever that this latter machine is the ONLY BSA twin on the collectors' market commanding phenomenally high prices, while the identically-engined, but later styled, Road Rocket sells for peanuts by comparison. This must be largely due to the RGS being alone in reverting to BSA's very much nicer mid-1950s styling.

Once this was my own Gold Flash of 1954 vintage. The beige seat cover and paint scheme cost extra

BSA refused to supply sidecar lugs on their mid 1950s swinging-arm frames. This led them to continue production of the otherwise obsolete semi-unit-construction engined plunger version for several more years

Above
The 1955 Shooting Star full springer came along as a much improved replacement for the old plunger Star Twin. However, the full-width Ariel-type wheel hubs, as used from 1956 onwards, began the decline

Above left
My own current 650 is an early 1954 version, one of the very few to have escaped export

Below left
Beauty, I know, lies in the eye of the beholder, and yes it's my bike again, but I still feel that this model year was THE nicest looking and also the best all-rounder that BSA ever made

Right
The Shooting Star's mildly tuned engine benefited greatly from having a cast-alloy cylinder head, which allowed it to run cooler than its predecessor and on higher piston compression ratios

Above
BSA's stylists never could leave well alone. Just look at those ultra-heavy, yet even less efficient, 1959-type cast-iron brake hubs and that ugly headlamp nacelle

Above right
America's market received this Gold Star competition-framed 650 Spitfire road scrambler from 1959 onwards. It had a smaller-capacity tank than standard and the single-cylinder scrambler's seat, etc

Below right
As if to confuse, the American market Flash used a 500 cc engine in 1959, not BSA's traditional 650

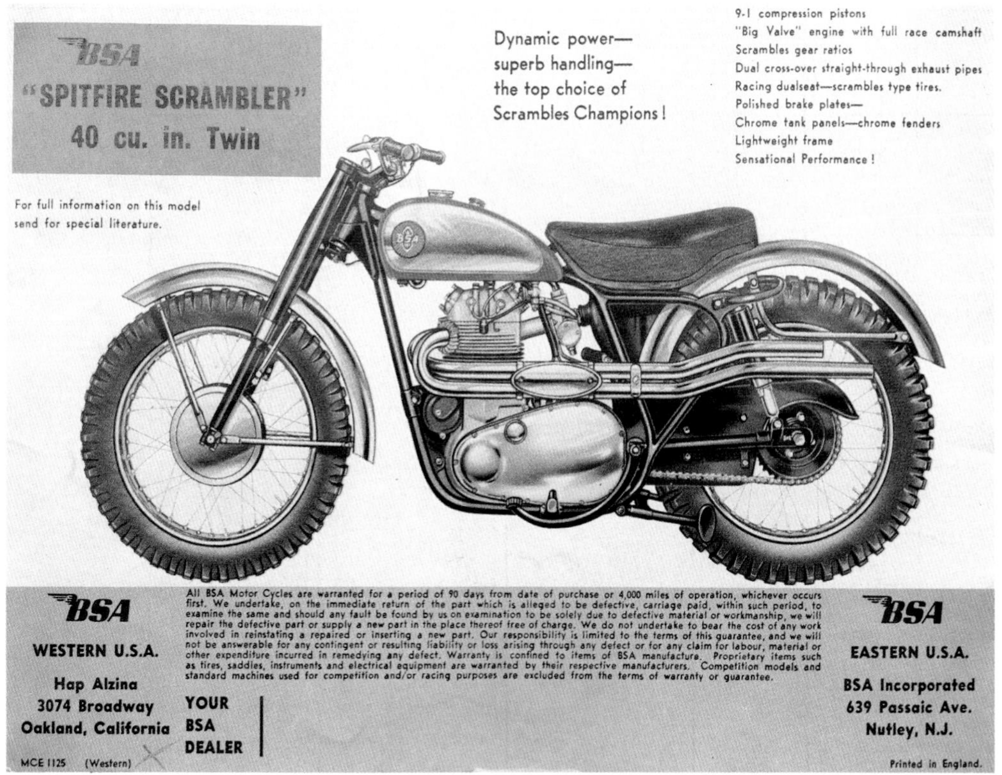
BSA
"SPITFIRE SCRAMBLER"
40 cu. in. Twin
Dynamic power—
superb handling—
the top choice of
Scrambles Champions!
9-1 compression pistons
"Big Valve" engine with full race camshaft
Scrambles gear ratios
Dual cross-over straight-through exhaust pipes
Racing dualseat—scrambles type tires.
Polished brake plates—
Chrome tank panels—chrome fenders
Lightweight frame
Sensational Performance!
For full information on this model send for special literature.
BSA
WESTERN U.S.A.
Hap Alzina
3074 Broadway
Oakland, California
All BSA Motor Cycles are warranted for a period of 90 days from date of purchase or 4,000 miles of operation, whichever occurs first. We undertake, on the immediate return of the part which is alleged to be defective, carriage paid, within such period, to examine the same and should any fault be found by us on examination to be solely due to defective material or workmanship, we will repair the defective part or supply a new part in the place thereof free of charge. We do not undertake to bear the cost of any work involved in reinstating a repaired or inserting a new part. Our responsibility is limited to the terms of this guarantee, and we will not be answerable for any contingent or resulting liability or loss arising through any defect or for any claim for labour, material or other expenditure incurred in remedying any defect. Warranty is confined to items of BSA manufacture. Proprietary items such as tires, saddles, instruments and electrical equipment are warranted by their respective manufacturers. Competition models and standard machines used for competition and/or racing purposes are excluded from the terms of warranty or guarantee.
YOUR
BSA
DEALER
BSA
EASTERN U.S.A.
BSA Incorporated
639 Passaic Ave.
Nutley, N.J.
MCE 1125 (Western)
Printed in England.

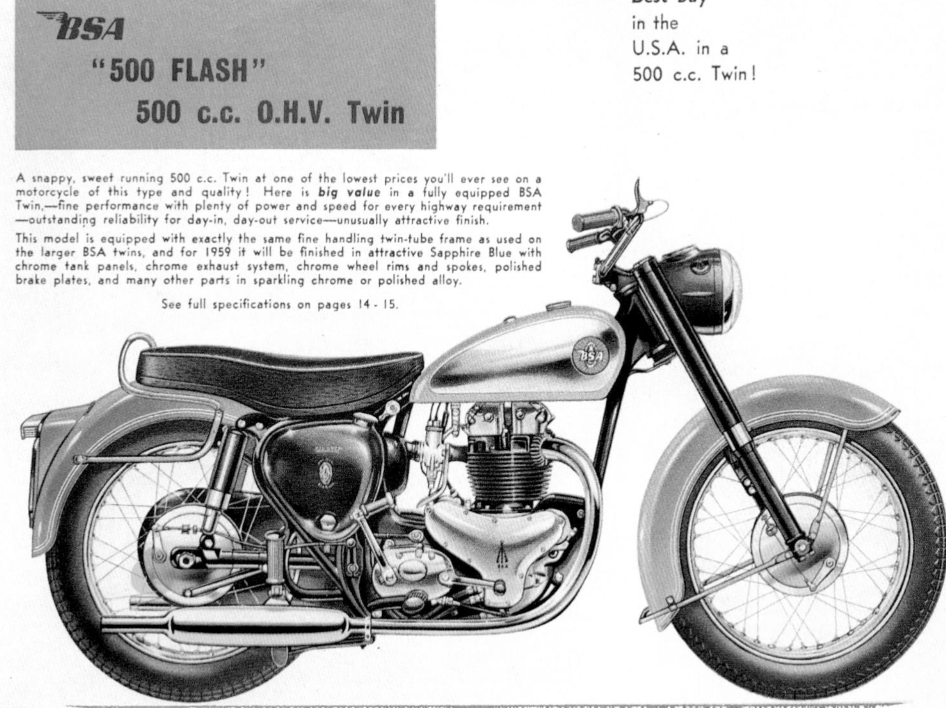
BSA
"500 FLASH"
500 c.c. O.H.V. Twin
Best buy
in the
U.S.A. in a
500 c.c. Twin!
A snappy, sweet running 500 c.c. Twin at one of the lowest prices you'll ever see on a motorcycle of this type and quality! Here is big value in a fully equipped BSA Twin,—fine performance with plenty of power and speed for every highway requirement—outstanding reliability for day-in, day-out service—unusually attractive finish.
This model is equipped with exactly the same fine handling twin-tube frame as used on the larger BSA twins, and for 1959 it will be finished in attractive Sapphire Blue with chrome tank panels, chrome exhaust system, chrome wheel rims and spokes, polished brake plates, and many other parts in sparkling chrome or polished alloy.
See full specifications on pages 14 - 15.

Above

Getting it right again in 1963 with the limited-edition 650 cc Rocket Gold Star. This could be purchased as seen here, in Clubmans race trim, or as a Sports Tourer

Right

The tuned 650 cc Super Rocket engines graced the Rocket Gold Stars later. Note the 1960 period extras, including front and rear crash bars, leopardskin seat cover, etc, but no crash hats for the riders

Above
Another RGS of 1963 vintage and with the high handlebar and forward footrest settings that are more sensible for road use. Chrome plated fork shrouds and rear swinging arm, as on this bike, were not among BSA's own options

Right
Just as a Touring RGS should be, or almost, for at the time this was my bike and I had chosen to mix the possible handlebar-to-footrest options for maximum personal comfort

BSA

C15, B40 and B25

By the mid 1950s, BSA's long-running and basically pre-war-designed 250 cc four-stroke-engined C10L and C11G (side and ohv) commuter bikes were becoming uneconomical to produce, but instead of starting afresh, the company looked around within the group for a cheaper and more easily built alternative.

The old 'C' range cost problem was due to its separate engine and gearbox construction, meaning that there were as many powerplant and chassis parts for plating, painting, casting, welding and machining as on the more expensive B31 heavyweight. Yet the smaller bike obviously needed to be sold at a much lower price.

Small Heath's answer was to 'borrow' Edward Turner's 149 cc Terrier and 199 cc Cub unit-construction design from Triumph, their wholly-owned subsidiary. By considerably strengthening it and enlarging the cylinder capacity to 247 cc, they produced their own C15 engine, which was physically smaller than its predecessor. This, in turn, allowed the use of a lighter and cheaper to produce chassis.

The idea certainly worked well, and tens of thousands bought these little bikes, which were faster, lighter, sportier and, in real terms, cheaper than either their rivals or predecessors. They were also much stronger mechanically than even Turner's Cub, which could often prove fragile.

Most new C15s were bought by youngsters and learners, who not only learned their first riding skills on them, but also the black art of home maintenance without the right (if any!) spanners. Sadly, this has since brought these smashing little bikes a rather poor, yet quite unwarranted, reputation.

Remember, this was BSA's first four-stroke engine not to use gaskets between the inner and outer timing covers, or to seal the primary chaincase, and it broke new ground through its extensive use of Phillips cross-head screws. The last led many bodge artists without the right tools to resort to using a hammer and chisel.

Considerable harm was done to C15s by those who couldn't afford the right tools, or didn't read the maintenance manual, or attempted chiseling off left-hand-threaded nuts which would have undone easily had the miscreants only realized that they were tightening not loosening.

That the C15s were and, indeed, are very fine and well engineered bikes is perhaps best proven by the vast number of successes the Trials (C15T) and Scrambles (C15S) models have scored over the years. These include winning the ultra-tough Scottish Six Days Trial twice and many world Moto-X honours.

It was such a strong engine design that BSA were able to stretch its capacity to 343 cc for the B40, then on to 440 cc to become the B44 Victor and finally to

Humble the C10/11 series might once have seemed, but a generation of riders went to work or play on just such machines as this 1947 C11, enjoying its near absolute reliability

An almost 100 per cent standard unit-construction C15 of 1959, merely missing one air cleaner hose rubber, although judging from the forward lean, its kick starter has seen better days

499 cc as the B50. In this form, the engine won two 500 cc Moto-X World Championships, which couldn't be bad for what had actually originated as Triumph's 149 cc Terrier.

The B40 (343 cc) version didn't arrive officially until November 1960 for 1961 production, but I encountered it in May 1960 when, in my role as a *Motor Cycle News* staff man, I happened to visit Small Heath to pick up a bike to use as personal transport for the following week's Isle of Man TT races. Borrowing and reporting on new bikes was then, as now, something of a TT week tradition, but I was far from amused when they wheeled out what I thought was a mere 250, not least as it was a very long way to Liverpool and I also happened to be taking my wife to the Island. BSA's man soon explained, however, that this was not a 250, but a prototype 350, which went some way to lessen my worries. He claimed it to be capable of a 500's performance (it was, too!), and although he didn't, he might also have rightly added that it had a 250's weight and size.

Perhaps Small Heath's mistake with the B40, if any, was in phasing out the old heavyweights a little too quickly, for left suddenly, as they were, without any choice, many traditionalists shunned the B40 without giving it a chance. The British Army, however, who were not nearly as interested in fashion, did buy B40s by the thousand and used them right up until 1989.

As for the 1967-on 250 cc B25 Barracuda, whose new and untried engine supplanted the by then well sorted C15G powerplant, I can only suggest that it was one of BSA's very few aberrations. At the time, it certainly cost them dear in guarantee claims.

The problem was that someone at BSA decided to considerably increase this engine's performance and, at the same time, changed the previous race-proven roller big-end for car-type split shell bearings. These, as it turned out, would not stand the hammer.

Left
This original-specification competition C15T never has been trialed, so it must be almost unique. It was restored by Brian Moore

Right
I wouldn't mind a pound for every leg burn inflicted by C15T exhaust pipes. We privateer trials riders soon altered the pipe run to tuck inside, rather than outside, the frame. BSA eventually followed suit, too

Below
The nearside of Brian Moore's C15T, and equally faultless. The bike was too heavy as supplied, even for 1959's trials season

BSA
OIL LEVEL
B.S.A. MOTOR CYCLES LTD
BIRMINGHAM
250

Right

A sporty SS80 of 1967 vintage, restored by John Warrilow. Fortunately, mechanical spares are still reasonably plentiful, not so such items as the toolbox and oil tank transfers

Below

1967's engine was of the 'F' type, meaning its internal design had almost reached B44 Victor specification except, that is, outright capacity and the still plain timing-side main bearing. The final all-roller-bearing transformation came later that year with the 'G' suffix

BSA
SPORT
STAR
VNP 854 G

BSA

Above
Former World Trials Champion Martin Lampkin riding a recent Classic Scottish. He is mounted on the works C15T ridden in 1967 by Alan, his older brother, who was victorious in that year's full International Six Days event

Left
One of the very last military B40s built, and not completely phased out of British Army service until late 1988

Right
Unlike the military jobs, civilian B40s always retained the earlier frame and a smaller-capacity fuel tank with C15-style badges. This bike was built around 1961

Opposite
B25 and last of the line. It had a Victor-type frame, alloy cylinder barrel, downdraught carburettor, much more performance, etc, but was spoiled by the lack of a decent engine oil filter to protect its split shell big-end from circulating swarf. Consequently, most suffered regularly from bearing failures

The swinging-arm Gold Stars

Perhaps one of THE most interesting machines to compete in the 1952 Senior (International) TT was a supposedly home-brewed BSA special, entered and ridden by Roland Pike. However, as far as the motorcycle magazines were concerned, no one would have known, for this bike didn't even rate a mention in their reports.

This was quite an incredible omission, for Pike was particularly well known to the specialized journals, both for his track successes AND, in this instance, more importantly as a BSA employee whose responsibilities included developing experimental (works) Gold Stars for racing.

Pike's so-called 500 cc special was stamped as a ZB, but featured a cylinder head and barrel with larger fins together with the later BB type separate (as opposed to cast-in) rocker box. The last had been introduced already for the production 350s, but not the 500s. Although it might be excusable for that lot to escape notice, his bike's chassis also featured full swinging arm rear suspension.

So obvious a works prototype was it that one can only suggest the collusion of a virtual army of technical journalists in not giving it a mention, most especially as this duo were not entered in the Clubmans race, but more prominently in the World Championship counting Senior TT.

Pike didn't win, but he was lapping against the Gileras and Manxes at around 83 mph before his engine expired. On the other hand, Eric Housley and Bob McIntyre literally romped away with the Junior Clubmans, breaking lap and race records with their new plunger ZB Gold Stars, whose 350 cc engines also had BB top ends.

The resulting production swinging-arm BB types arrived by the end of that year for the 1953 season. Just as their predecessors, they were much hampered in UK Clubmans racing by being limited to low compression ratios forced by the low 72-octane (pool) petrol which still lingered on after the war.

Coincidentally, there was no longer a world fuel shortage at that time, and the British oil companies had long pleaded with our government to be allowed to offer higher octanes and better petrol blends, but the authorities wouldn't shift. As a result, even the new and better gas-flowed Gold Stars could only perform much as the old.

The eventual slight improvement to 80-octane came just in time for 1954's Isle of Man series, and brought a rash of Gold Star tuning improvements, including appreciably higher compression ratios. To keep the lid on, more crankcase-to-cylinder head through-bolts were added, whereas the engine's overall height was also lowered by shortening the con-rod.

First of the swinging-arm BBs, which gave very much more tractable road performance than the later CBs and DBDs

Above

Rare as rocking-horse manure this one, a genuine, unrestored International Six Days Trial BB34 of 1954 – exactly as it was prepared originally by BSA's competition department

Left

The other side of the same ISDT machine, showing some of the large number of works modifications. These include a Lucas waterproof 'wader' Magdynamo, a centre stand mounted further forward so that the machine balances better for rapid wheel removal, and a high-pressure air bottle for tyres. Even the event scrutineers' paint and wire seals are still intact. All in all, a fabulous piece of history

Above
What a pair of beauties, a brace of 350 cc DBs dating from 1956 and 1961, photographed fittingly at Greg-na-baa, right by the TT course

Above right
Roger Neale piloting his 1959 DB 500 scrambler to yet another victory, this time in 1989 and at the Pre-65 Moto-X Club's Frensham International. Note more modern telescopic forks and AMC front brake hub

Below right
Taken in 1980, although it could easily have been during the late 1950s, and doesn't this DBD rider look the part?

A larger drive side main bearing was substituted to improve crankshaft rigidity, and as this required a different drive-side engine casting, BSA chose to make it an even more bulletproof assembly by incorporating extra internal strengthening ridges from around the main bearing.

Incidentally, virtually all of BSA's road race development was done on the 350 cc engines first. Then, if a modification worked, it was transferred, often at a much later date, to the 500s. Thus, although the former briefly adopted oval flywheels to become the CB model, the latter continued as a BB for a little while longer.

The 1955 season was particularly confusing for Gold Star engine number prefixes, not least as the racers rapidly passed through being CBs to DBs without much of a change. The old BB engine versions also lived on for touring and scrambles in some known instances until a year later.

The final racing 500s carried a DBD prefix, which related merely to a larger inlet port and wider carburettor fixing stud spacing to allow for the fitting of Amal's larger-bore ($1\frac{1}{2}$ in.) Grand Prix instrument. The smaller (350 cc capacity) engines continued as DBs, however, because their carburettor was already quite large enough.

Although some Gold Stars were still being turned out to special order as late as 1963, in development terms, those 1957 models were really the end of the line. There was little point in BSA striving for more speed after that year, as the Clubmans TT, which was always the object of the exercise, had itself been abandoned.

Generally, the best models for road use were always the 350s, not least because they were, and are, very much less fussy and also appreciably easier to start. However, perhaps better still are the even softer-tune BB series 500s which, in touring rather than race trim, have the cooking B33's manners with Goldie looks and slightly better performance than even the above-mentioned 350s.

One particularly sobering thought, in view of the phenomenal prices being asked for Gold Stars today, is that for a really good 350 DB version to reach 105 mph (or a DBD 500, 112 mph), it takes ultra-close and tall gear ratios, a very uncomfortable dropped handlebar position, totally anti-social carburettors and silencing, etc, whereas BSA's humble and much lower-priced A10 does it all so much more easily through having more cubes!

Almost 30 years on and Don Ellis on a virtually standard DB 350, racing through Ballacraine on the Isle of Man's TT course

Early 1960s and Don Ellis racing his very special 'oil-in-frame' 350 cc Gold Star which, at one time, also used a home-built short-stroke 250 engine

Pete Cottrell on his Grand Prix racing-specification (as opposed to Clubmans) DB 350, with central oil tank and five-gallon fuel tank, etc, but a non-standard front brake

Above and right

A late DBD 34 model seen in all its glory, still ready to race, but hopelessly impractical for road use

A-group unit twins

The year 1962 brought the introduction of the all-new A50 and A65 unit-construction 500 and 650 cc twins, of which Bert Hopwood (who designed the original pre-unit 650s) says, in his book, *Whatever happened to the British Motor Cycle Industry?*: 'they were but a deterioration of what had been a well proven product'.

Assuming that there was no malice in this statement, he above all should know, of course, although these machines were conceived at a time when Hopwood was working for, and being loyal to, Triumph. At the time, the latter's entire management, Hopwood included, were being messed about considerably by their masters at Small Heath, as illustrated amply in the same book.

Certainly true is that Hopwood's low-compression-ratio, soft-cam-profile original A10 was designed and built to run on low-octane pool petrol, which was all that was available at the time. This, surely, must have also been a factor in why it was the smoothest and least vibration-prone of all BSA's long-running big twins.

That is about as far down the Hopwood line as I would personally go, however, for although BSA were admittedly not so lucky on the early unit models, since they rushed them into production after too short a pre-production test and gestation period, they did eventually sort out all of the bugs.

Given, too, that the love or hate affair between rider and any motorcycle is brought about by the total sum of the parts, not merely an engine, I would contend that the SOFT-tune versions of the later unit twins were arguably tougher, just as smooth, were a vital 2 in. shorter in wheelbase, had much better front forks and generally displayed far superior handling to Hopwood's A10.

Vibration could certainly be a bit of a problem on the hot jobs, but prior to 1970's diabolical Umberslade Hall frame versions, no better or worse than on any other manufacturer's equivalent. Until Yamaha's much later vibration-damping, contra-rotating balance shaft efforts, this was the inevitable price paid by ALL vertical twins for having an unbalanced design.

More cubes, or a higher state of tune, HAD to add up to even greater vibration. This is precisely why Hopwood's Flash and the unit equivalent base model A65s were always much sweeter than, say, the Rocket Gold Star or the various late Spitfires. This applies equally, regardless of the method of engine construction.

A single-carburettor A65 Thunderbolt of 1967, and now with two-way front fork damping. It produced less vibration than the tuned, twin-carb Spitfires and Lightnings, and altogether was rather a nice bike

BSA
PHV 396E

Chris Vincent, seen here racing during the early 1960s at Brands Hatch, also won the International Sidecar TT with his unit BSA-powered outfit

Why BSA, and others, bothered modifying their vertical twins to ever higher states of tune is, of course, quite another matter, especially as they did this almost annually. As a result, they risked losing their proud record for outright reliability. This was chronicled by the era's press testers, who reported increasingly on instances of vibration causing metal fatigue and bits to fall off!

Most post-era pundits trot out the old explanatory line about it being the speed-crazed Americans' fault in their clamouring for more, but who were those mythical Yanks that the likes of BSA couldn't afford to ignore? As a one-time contributor and subscriber to several of that great country's motorcycling magazines, my own recollections are somewhat different.

Cycle World, for instance, when testing the 1964 super-tuned Spitfire Mk 2 version, strongly criticized the bike's vibration levels. They also stated that this model overheated badly, was difficult to start and suffered from poor carburation. This they found hardly surprising, as the US-spec. Mk 2s all came

Two carburettors, higher compression ratio, greater power, and vibration to match; that just about sums up the Lightning of the late 1960s

fitted with a pair of large-bore Amal GP race carburettors that were quite unsuited to road use.

Their list of complaints went on and on, and there was certainly no appreciation for the extra speed of this bike over its lower-tuned predecessor, let alone a request that BSA should keep tuning to give them some more. The shock waves of this negative test did reverberate back across the Atlantic, however, and rapidly resulted in the much nicer to ride and ordinarily carburated Spitfire Mk 3, so, might one ask who was, and is, kidding whom?

My own suspicions are that the oft-quoted 'speed-crazed American' theory was but a convenient scapegoat for the failure of the then BSA middle management to ever actually use their own products. No wonder the workforce got stroppy, because they did ride them and knew precisely what was going wrong. Sadly, their voice, like ours, went unheard until it was too late.

A Spitfire Mk 2 of 1966, surely one of BSA's best-ever lookers. However, those twin GP racing carburettors proved an expensive flop on the roadster

BSA
BSA

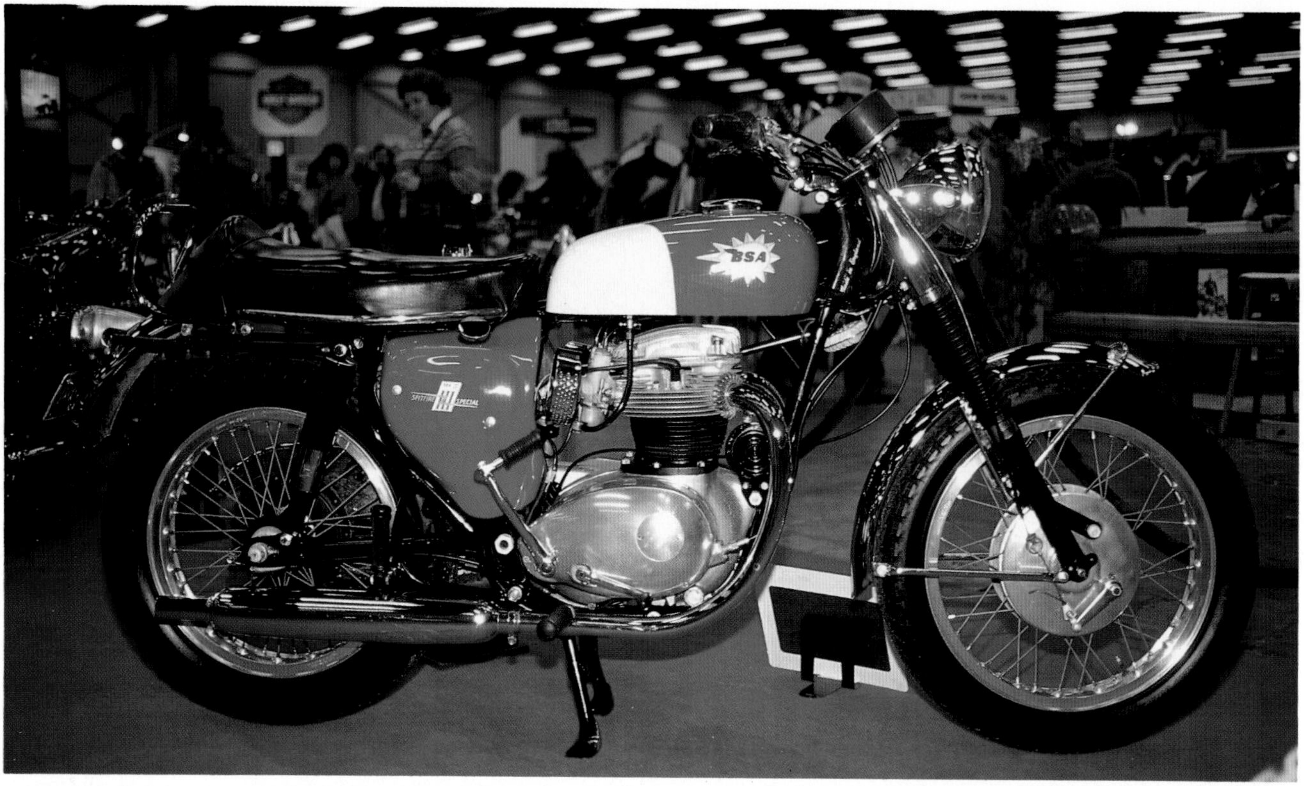
BSA
SPITFIRE
SPECIAL

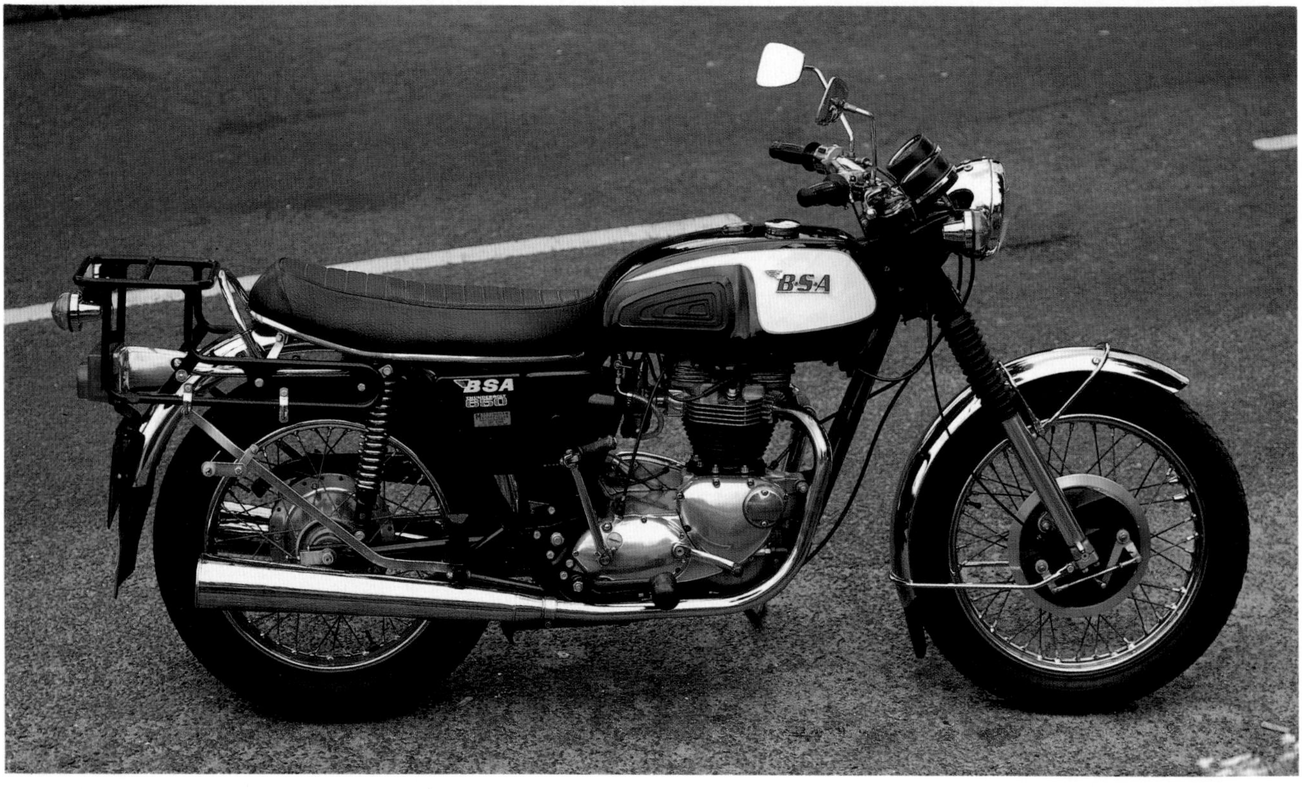
B·S·A
BSA
650

Above left
The small-fuel-tank, American-specification Spitfire Mk 3 Special, seen here at Atlanta's annual show

Below left
End of the line and now exceedingly rare, 1973's BSA T65 Thunderbolt was really a Triumph marketed under another name, or rather pirated by Small Heath

Right
Peter Hollinshead regularly rides this 1963 unit 650 in Moto-X races. To slim down the otherwise bulbous engine, he has chopped off the entire alternator assembly

Licensed to thrill

Those two James Bond film makers Harry Saltzman and Albert R. Broccoli needed a futuristic-looking motorcycle back in 1965, for use in a chase sequence between the baddies and '007' driving his rocket-launching, nail-throwing, ejector-seated Aston Martin. The bike chosen was one of BSA's then brand-new, unit-construction 650 cc Lightnings. This, too, was fitted with real rockets which were fired off in the film by the evil Spectre organization's lovely rider, played by the Italian actress Luciana Paluzzi, or at least supposedly by her, as she and the Lightning chased after Bond, attempting to zap both him and the Aston into oblivion.

Naturally, it couldn't turn out that way, otherwise there wouldn't have been any other money-spinning Bond films had he come to grief. It wasn't really Miss Paluzzi herself who did the riding or crashing, either, but the sidecar TT race star Chris Vincent, who also happened to work at BSA.

What supposedly happened when the Lightning's four rockets were fired off in mid-chase was that '007' merely flicked a switch which raised an armour-plated shield on the Aston, off which the missiles bounced harmlessly. Then, of course, it was Bond's turn to truly mangle the BSA.

Two dummy Lightnings stood by for this final destruction scene, being switched with the real one between takes just in time to crash into an apparently very deep lake. The genuine bike and the Aston were wheeled off to the sidelines and so lived to travel worldwide afterwards, promoting the film.

The Aston was eventually sold at auction and fetched over £100,000, being bought by a rich American collector. The bike, however, which had brought its makers' products so much extra international publicity, long lay unwanted at Pinewood Film Studios, forgotten and gathering dust.

It was finally given to W. P. (Tommy) Green, the famous special effects man who had been responsible for its rocket-firing conversion, and indeed most of the other similar gimmicks in *Thunderball.* He wasn't a motorcyclist, however, so the BSA would not be ridden again until years later, and only then when he passed away.

During 1983 it came up for sale by a motorcycle trader who was acting on behalf of the late Tommy Green's estate and was immediately snapped up by BSA enthusiast Neville Lewis. He rides it only very occasionally, hence its total mileage to date only being 1040, including all the filming, but boy does it vibrate!

Valve lifter levers, which are just visible on each side of the handlebars, operated pairs of hand-grenade-type percussion caps to actually ignite and fire the bike's rockets

The 1965 rocket-firing BSA Lightning used in the James Bond film Thunderball, *for which it carried a totally fictitious registration mark and was ridden by famous road racer Chris Vincent*

Victorious Victors

'So much to see you hardly know where to begin! But Scramblers will probably start with Jeff Smith's fabulous 420 cc job which won the World Moto Cross Crown', or so read the blurb for BSA's stand at London's 1964 Motor Cycle Show. The bike they referred to was really an overbored B40, the engine of which was about to be further enlarged to 441 cc as the production Victor MX Grand Prix.

Smith, you see, had clinched 1964's 14-race series World Moto-X title by winning seven, finishing second in six, and taking one third place when his bike suffered a puncture, which couldn't be bad for an engine whose origins could be traced right back to Triumph's 150 cc Terrier. His victories were certainly no fluke, either, for in 1965 Smith and the Victor went out and won all over again.

Motor Cycle magazine reported of the resulting bikes' 1964 for 1965 début: 'They have given Jeff Smith's all conquering 420 a name now', 'they' being BSA and the name? What else, but 'Victor'. In their innocence, *Motor Cycle* went on to say: 'Funny thing though it seems to have been upped to a 440 cc', which was almost right, since it had actually been stretched to a capacity of 441 cc.

Such engine capacity increases featured throughout the ensuing production Victor's short life, and started from the very moment that BSA's works riders realized they could often lap faster on the more nimble C15 Scrambles 250s than on their larger-capacity and faster, but far heavier, 500 cc Gold Stars. This resulted in Brian Martin, who was BSA's competition chief, overboring a 250 to 343 cc with considerable success.

Next a new crankshaft with a longer throw (90 mm as opposed to 70 mm) resulted in the 343 cc model becoming that all-conquering 420, while a set of meatier crankcases and a new cylinder barrel casting allowed for yet another overbore to 79 mm which gave 441 cc. That operation was later repeated when a final bore and stroke of 84 × 90 mm gave 499 cc.

What really counted in scrambling was that the Victors were still of 250 cc weight, wheelbase and size, so they were competing on level terms with the physically larger and heavier rival 500s whilst enjoying a considerable power-to-weight ratio bonus. Indeed, the production B44GP only weighed in at 255 lb when most of its rivals were anything up to 100 lb heavier and some 4 in. longer.

The first Victor roadster version was unveiled at the 1966 show. Other than its gearing, compression ratio, sundry road equipment and a separate oil tank (as opposed to carrying the engine's lubricating oil in the frame tubes), it virtually mirrored the Scrambler. Coming, as it did, from staid old BSA, this was quite a surprise.

Above right
1967's Victor road version, developed directly from Smith's 441 cc scrambler, now with the square-finned cylinder head and barrel, and fibreglass fuel tank plus side panels, etc

Below right
A works-specification ISDT Victor 441 of 1968, fitted with silencer, light, trials tyres and a slightly larger-capacity fuel tank

Below
Multi World Moto-X Champion Jeff Smith and his Victor, seen winning yet again at Halstead during June 1968

After all, here was a 250 cc-sized bike of all but 500 cc capacity with a wheelbase of 52 in., as opposed to the old B33's 56 in. and a wet weight of 336 lb compared to 440 lb. At the same time, it also enjoyed a considerable power boost from the original's 23 bhp (at 5500 rpm) to 29 bhp (at 5750 rpm). The result was BSA's first ever 'wheelie' machine!

There were some snags, or rather features that didn't compare quite as well. Most especially starting the new bike could often be more difficult due to Joe Lucas' often indifferent electrics, and even the physical smallness which made these machines so much fun to ride solo became less attractive when two up. Given a rider of normal build, there would be very little saddle room left for any size of passenger.

To me, as a regular off-road competitor, the Victors were, indeed still are, truly fantastic machines. In terms of fashion, however, perhaps they were just too far ahead of their time, for it took another decade and the Japanese to really cash in on what, by then, was the blossoming trail bike market, which should have been the Victor's ideal role.

70
BSA
Avon
Classic Bike
MAGAZINE
Castrol

The final 499 cc Victor B50s enjoyed considerable road racing success, as did this one which was ridden by David Duxbury to a class win at Daytona as recently as 1982

Above

Another International Six Days Trial 441 cc Victor, but this time an Eric Cheney-framed British Army Team machine. This was also fitted with a very interesting exhaust system, especially developed for the Army by Queens University, Belfast

Right

A 250 SS actually, but by the 1970s featuring the same awful styling as its bigger B50 brother, which BSA re-christened at one time as their newest Gold Star – what affrontery!

BSA
250SS

The glorious triples

Designed by Triumph for building at BSA, raced to phenomenal success on both sides of the Atlantic, and scuppered finally by a stock-market crash, aided by Britain's then government who were in cahoots with BSA's Norton Villiers rivals. That just about sums up the short story of Bert Hopwood and Doug Hele's Rocket 3 triples, but oh what fabulous bikes.

It all started back in the mid 1960s when the 'superbike' cult was just in its infancy. Hopwood, who was BSA/Triumph's chief designer, recognized that they would need a new engine giving at least 60 bhp if the group was to stay in the ball park, yet there was neither the time left nor any money available for designing or developing anything fresh.

Hopwood might conceivably have got there by upping the capacity of an existing Triumph or BSA twin from 650 to 750 cc, but only at the expense of poor crankshaft balance and, hence, even worse vibration. Instead, he and Hele came up with the novel idea of grafting an extra cylinder on to Triumph's smaller 493 cc Daytona twin engine to turn it into a 740 cc triple.

A slight over simplification, perhaps, but this really is how Triumph's T750 Trident and BSA's Rocket 3 came about. They were only styled and badged differently because the BSA and Triumph halves of the group employed separate and rival North American importers, who might not have taken to either version had these bikes looked too much alike.

Fortunately, the Americans did like them. Indeed, one early export batch of BSA machines were taken virtually straight from the crate to Daytona's famous Speed Bowl where they lapped at an incredible 131.723 mph. Then they went on to complete what would have been the Daytona 200's full 200-mile race distance at a 123 mph average, proving themselves the world's fastest production machines at the time.

Britain had to wait for her triples until the resulting export backlog was satiated, but the weekly newspaper *Motor Cycle* was loaned what would be a home-market specification machine during September 1968. They reported a somewhat lower mean maximum and a highest one-way speed of 122 mph, which was well down on those American Daytona bikes' speeds, but they were still real arm wrenchers that just cried out to be raced.

BSA, meanwhile, had steadfastly resisted any road race involvement ever since the early 1920s (at least officially!), but now they were being pressurized to have a real go by the combined US importers as 1970's actual Daytona 200 race approached. The bikes had already proved that they could stay the distance at speeds that were quite high enough.

Gene Romero's works-prepared Triumph triple took pole position for the race at an incredible 157.34 mph, and he was followed closely by the similarly mounted Gary Nixon and then Mike Hailwood on the first Rocket 3.

The engine department of 1969's Mk 1 Rocket 3 in all of its original glory, and ready to power Britain's first truly arm-wrenching Superbike

Same model triple, but a different machine, complete with the high-rise type of handlebars so beloved Stateside

BSA/Triumph however, had not allowed sufficient time for development and quite minor mechanical gremlins sidelined Messrs Hailwood and Nixon when they were actually leading quite easily.

With more time to get ready for 1971's race, Doug Hele redesigned the camshafts to give increased lift with longer opening times. He also mounted the contact breaker remotely on roller bearings to reduce flex and maintain accurate ignition timing (which had caused most of 1970's problems). At the same time, he upped the bike's compression ratio to 12:1 whilst reworking the combustion chamber's shape.

Rob North chipped in by building a batch of ultra-light (35 lb) frames with a steeper (64°) steering head angle, while the engine was mounted 1 in. higher for improved cornering clearance (although the rider's seat was actually lower). Although there were never any official figures released, the resulting 1971 race bikes were reckoned to give a then quite staggering 82–83 bhp at 8200–8500 rpm and yet be even easier to ride.

Those fabulous BSA/Triumph triples scored an easy 1-2-3 on their return to

Daytona, this time with Dick Mann's and Don Emde's Rockets sandwiching Gene Romero's Triumph. There was even better to come at the big prize money international Race of the Year in England, where John Cooper's BSA triple literally thrashed Giacomo Agostini and his previously unbeatable MV Agusta Grand Prix Team.

Over 100,000 people cheered themselves hoarse on that day, which must go down as one of THE greatest in all of racing's long history. However, it must also have been something of a double-edged sword for Messrs Hopwood and Hele, as those winning engines had only been intended as temporary measures for limited stop-gap production while they worked on a new and even better modular-construction ohc range of powerplants.

Had BSA's management given the go-ahead, there would have already been a high-tech 200 cc base engine whose main components could have been multiplied as required, almost ad infinitum through 400/600/800/1000 cc, etc, to power BSA/Triumph's entire 1970s and 1980s ranges. The problem, however, following the triples' racing successes, was that BSA decided that neither they, nor we, needed anything better, whereas the Japanese soon proved otherwise.

The Mk 2 version of BSA's Rocket was easily distinguishable by the conical wheel hubs and cheap wire mudguard stays. It was nicknamed by most as the 'comical 'ub' model, not least because it was hardly an improvement

BSA
ROCKET THREE

Above

Dick Mann at Daytona, on the works BSA he used in 1971 to thrash all comers in the annual 200-mile race

Right

Mann's works-entered Daytona 200 winner featured a Rob North frame and had been extensively breathed on by BSA/Triumph's tuning and development ace Doug Hele. This combination may well have continued winning for many more years had BSA's management not made the excuse that they needed the race shop's workforce to do other things and hence pulled the plug

29
BSA Rocket3
5
AP Lockheed

Left
John 'Mooneyes' Cooper beat the Grand Prix might of Agostini and his Italian MV on this bike, and over 100,000 partisans almost lost their voices cheering him on at the Race of the Year

Below
David Roper is still winning races on the ex-Dick Mann machine, including numerous later victories at Classic Daytona

SAMMY MILLER MOTOR CYCLE MUSEUM
BSA
MC1

Still-born and specials

Above

The only survivor from two very special Triumph-powered works machines ridden to success by BSA's Arthur and Alan Lampkin in the 1966 ISDT. Their engines were basically 500 cc Daytonas, but with single instead of twin carburettors and cast-aluminium cylinder barrels. whereas chassis were similar to the Victor's

Left

BSA's futuristic 250 cc four-valve MC 1 'world beater', as designed by Doug Hele during 1950 and successfully tested by Geoff Duke in 1953. Then it was cancelled because Bert Hopwood could not, or would not, give BSA's board a promise that it would definitely win first time out

113T

Above
BSA weren't the only ones who could build specials. Witness this stretched and double 650 cc engined job spotted outside the Boot Hill Saloon in Daytona, where its owner had no doubt paused to sample the waters

Left
Arthur Lampkin in the actual event held in Sweden. BSA/Triumph's much later production Adventurer/Trophy trail models were derived from these prototypes

Left

BSA/Triumph's prototype ohc-engined Bandit had been designed for the Group by Edward Turner, but sadly its engine proved to be far too fragile and cost a fortune in development before finally being shelved

Below

BSA spent vast sums of money buying the British manufacturing rights to inventor Felix Wankel's rotary engine. Despite its badges, however, this bike is really a DKW built in Germany rather than Small Heath